牛津语言学入门丛书

丛书主编 H.G.Widdowson

Semantics

语 义 学

A.P.Cowie 著

上海外语教育出版社

外教社 SHANGHAI FOREIGN LANGUAGE EDUCATION PRESS

图书在版编目（CIP）数据

语义学：英文 / （英）考伊（Cowie, A. P.）著.
—上海：上海外语教育出版社，2012（2020重印）
（牛津语言学入门丛书）

ISBN 978-7-5446-2765-8

Ⅰ．①语… Ⅱ．①考… Ⅲ．①语义学－英文 Ⅳ．①H030

中国版本图书馆CIP数据核字（2012）第064111号

图字：09-2011-691号

出版发行：上海外语教育出版社

（上海外国语大学内）　邮编：200083
电　　话：021-65425300（总机）
电子邮箱：bookinfo@sflep.com.cn
网　　址：http://www.sflep.com
责任编辑：蔡一鸣

印　　刷：上海信老印刷厂
开　　本：850×1168　1/32　印张4.75　字数148千字
版　　次：2012年5月第1版　2020年9月第6次印刷
印　　数：1 100册

书　　号：ISBN 978-7-5446-2765-8 / H·1336
定　　价：16.00元

本版图书如有印装质量问题，可向本社调换
质量服务热线：4008-213-263　电子邮箱：editorial@sflep.com

出 版 前 言

在语言研究方面不乏详尽权威的导论。但这些学术专论都趋于冗长且学术性太强，对初学者来说大有泰山压顶之势。于是，"牛津语言学入门丛书"，这套让人们循序渐进、轻松地掌握复杂概念的过渡性简明教程，就应运而生了。

人们在对语言的特定细节进行剖析之前，应该对语言整体有个大致的了解。作为语言学研究方向的学生进行深入研究之前的热身阅读，这套丛书的主旨是为人们理解那些学术性强的语言学专著奠定理论基础。因为这套丛书浅显易懂，对那些感兴趣却并非专门从事语言研究的人进一步了解语言也大有裨益。

本套丛书采用了统一的结构模式，在"前言"之后，由"概述"、"阅读材料"、"参考书目"和"术语表"四个部分构成。第一部分概述是全书的主体，也是有关该领域研究的导论。第二部分提供与书中各章节内容相应的深入阅读的材料，其后所附的问题极具启发性，有助于读者形成对有关领域研究的独立见解。第三部分提供相应章节的参考书目，并对它们的主要内容作了点评，以便有兴趣的学习者深入学习。第四部分列出术语表，帮助初学者了解有关术语的定义。

本套丛书的读者对象是英语专业高年级学生、语言学、应用语言学与相关专业研究生以及对相应领域感兴趣的人员。欢迎读者对我们的工作提出宝贵意见。

Semantics

A.P. Cowie is Honorary Reader
in Lexicography at the University
of Leeds.

Oxford Introductions to Language Study

Series Editor H.G. Widdowson

Semantics

A.P. Cowie

OXFORD

UNIVERSITY PRESS

OXFORD
UNIVERSITY PRESS

Great Clarendon Street, Oxford OX2 6DP

Oxford University Press is a department of the University of Oxford.
It furthers the University's objective of excellence in research, scholarship,
and education by publishing worldwide in

Oxford New York

Auckland Cape Town Dar es Salaam Hong Kong Karachi
Kuala Lumpur Madrid Melbourne Mexico City Nairobi
New Delhi Shanghai Taipei Toronto

With offices in

Argentina Austria Brazil Chile Czech Republic France Greece
Guatemala Hungary Italy Japan Poland Portugal Singapore
South Korea Switzerland Thailand Turkey Ukraine Vietnam

OXFORD and OXFORD ENGLISH are registered trade marks of
Oxford University Press in the UK and in certain other countries

For Cabu

Contents

Preface

Purpose

What justification might there be for a series of introductions to language study? After all, linguistics is already well served with introductory texts: expositions and explanations which are comprehensive, authoritative, and excellent in their way. Generally speaking, however, their way is the essentially academic one of providing a detailed initiation into the discipline of linguistics, and they tend to be lengthy and technical: appropriately so, given their purpose. But they can be quite daunting to the novice. There is also a need for a more general and gradual introduction to language: transitional texts which will ease people into an understanding of complex ideas. This series of introductions is designed to serve this need.

Their purpose, therefore, is not to supplant but to support the more academically oriented introductions to linguistics: to prepare the conceptual ground. They are based on the belief that it is an advantage to have a broad map of the terrain sketched out before one considers its more specific features on a smaller scale, a general context in reference to which the detail makes sense. It is sometimes the case that students are introduced to detail without it being made clear what it is a detail *of*. Clearly, a general understanding of ideas is not sufficient: there needs to be closer scrutiny. But equally, close scrutiny can be myopic and meaningless unless it is related to the larger view. Indeed it can be said that the precondition of more particular enquiry is an awareness of what, in general, the particulars are about. This series is designed to provide this large-scale view of different areas of language study. As such it can serve as preliminary to (and precondition for) the more specific and specialized enquiry which students of linguistics are required to undertake.

But the series is not only intended to be helpful to such students. There are many people who take an interest in language without being academically engaged in linguistics *per se*. Such people may recognize the importance of understanding language for their own lines of enquiry, or for their own practical purposes, or quite simply for making them aware of something which figures so centrally in their everyday lives. If linguistics has revealing and relevant things to say about language, this should presumably not be a privileged revelation, but one accessible to people other than linguists. These books have been so designed as to accommodate these broader interests too: they are meant to be introductions to language more generally as well as to linguistics as a discipline.

Design

The books in the series are all cut to the same basic pattern. There are four parts: Survey, Readings, References, and Glossary.

Survey

This is a summary overview of the main features of the area of language study concerned: its scope and principles of enquiry, its basic concerns and key concepts. These are expressed and explained in ways which are intended to make them as accessible as possible to people who have no prior knowledge or expertise in the subject. The Survey is written to be readable and is uncluttered by the customary scholarly references. In this sense, it is simple. But it is not simplistic. Lack of specialist expertise does not imply an inability to understand or evaluate ideas. Ignorance means lack of knowledge, not lack of intelligence. The Survey, therefore, is meant to be challenging. It draws a map of the subject area in such a way as to stimulate thought and to invite a critical participation in the exploration of ideas. This kind of conceptual cartography has its dangers of course: the selection of what is significant, and the manner of its representation, will not be to the liking of everybody, particularly not, perhaps, to some of those inside the discipline. But these surveys are written in the belief that there must be an alternative to a technical account on the one hand and an idiot's guide on the other if linguistics is to be made relevant to people in the wider world.

Readings

Some people will be content to read, and perhaps re-read, the summary Survey. Others will want to pursue the subject and so will use the Survey as the preliminary for more detailed study. The Readings provide the necessary transition. For here the reader is presented with texts extracted from the specialist literature. The purpose of these Readings is quite different from the Survey. It is to get readers to focus on the specifics of what is said, and how it is said, in these source texts. Questions are provided to further this purpose: they are designed to direct attention to points in each text, how they compare across texts, and how they deal with the issues discussed in the Survey. The idea is to give readers an initial familiarity with the more specialist idiom of the linguistics literature, where the issues might not be so readily accessible, and to encourage them into close critical reading.

References

One way of moving into more detailed study is through the Readings. Another is through the annotated References in the third section of each book. Here there is a selection of works (books and articles) for further reading. Accompanying comments indicate how these deal in more detail with the issues discussed in the different chapters of the Survey.

Glossary

Certain terms in the Survey appear in bold. These are terms used in a special or technical sense in the discipline. Their meanings are made clear in the discussion, but they are also explained in the Glossary at the end of each book. The Glossary is cross-referenced to the Survey, and therefore serves at the same time as an index. This enables readers to locate the term and what it signifies in the more general discussion, thereby, in effect, using the Survey as a summary work of reference.

Use

The series has been designed so as to be flexible in use. Each title is separate and self-contained, with only the basic format in common. The four sections of the format, as described here, can be drawn upon and combined in different ways, as required by the needs, or interests, of different readers. Some may be content with the Survey and the Glossary and may not want to follow up the suggested References. Some may not wish to venture into the Readings. Again, the Survey might be considered as appropriate preliminary reading for a course in applied linguistics or teacher education, and the Readings more appropriate for seminar discussion during the course. In short, the notion of an introduction will mean different things to different people, but in all cases the concern is to provide access to specialist knowledge and stimulate an awareness of its significance. This series as a whole has been designed to provide this access and promote this awareness in respect to different areas of language study.

H. G. WIDDOWSON

Author's preface

This introductory book offers a short but comprehensive treatment of lexical semantics. It includes the study of the meaningful relationships between words, and the processes, among them metaphor, by which new words and new senses are developed. But it also embraces phraseology, a rapidly expanding area of study; the processes by which complex words (derivatives and compounds) are formed from simple words; and the analysis of words into meaningful components (such as 'adult' and 'non-adult'). In a final chapter there is discussion of the use of large corpora in lexical research and in dictionary-making.

I owe thanks to a number of people for help and encouragement at various stages in the book's progress. My thanks go first to Henry Widdowson, who has been a constant source of editorial support, exacting but also stimulating, from the very beginning. Second, I wish to thank Cristina Whitecross at Oxford University Press, both for her friendship and for help in improving the manuscript in its later stages. I am grateful, also, to Julia Sallabank, who earlier on gave much practical guidance. Above all, I wish to thank my wife Cabu for secretarial support and constant encouragement.

Survey

1

Words and meanings

'When I use a word', Humpty Dumpty said, in rather
a scornful tone, 'it means just what I choose it to mean
neither more nor less.'
'The question is', said Alice, 'whether you can make words
mean so many different things.'

(Lewis Carroll. *Alice through the Looking Glass. Macmillan
1871*)

What words mean is not always easy to pin down. Meanings
change over time, and people often use the same words to mean
different things. But Alice was wise to be cautious, because
Humpty Dumpty was wide of the mark. We should not be misled
by the constant expansion of the vocabulary of English, or by the
evident fact that individual words develop new meanings, into
thinking that we can make any word mean anything we like.
Apart from anything else, if the meaning is to be recognized by
somebody else, it has to be related to an existing sense in some
way or other. Words mean certain things by convention and this
we have to respect, to some degree at least, if we want to put
language to effective communicative use.

A second factor which limits the freedom we have to create
new meanings—whether idiosyncratic or not—is a strong dis-
position on the part of speakers, when faced with a recurring
situation or event, to deal with it in familiar language. Creativity
in our use of words tends to be reserved for special occasions.
By contrast, much-used words in well-worn meanings—often
within conventional phrases—reflect our most ordinary domestic routines. We 'lay the table', 'dry the dishes', 'take in the mail',
and 'put out the cat'.

As ordinary speakers of a language, of course, we are constantly brought up against our ignorance of specific meanings of **simple words**—those that consist of only one meaningful part (words in English like *glitch*, *butt*, *cypher*, *dross*, and so on). One reason for our difficulty is that leaving aside **onomatopoeic words**—those which like *cuckoo* and *rattle* are formed from a sound associated with the thing or action they refer to—the shapes of simple words, what they sound like or look like in writing, do not resemble what they mean.

The same point can be made with reference to words in other languages. *Fromage*, partly because of the long 'aah' and soft 'g' at the end, sounds much softer than *cheese*—a point that advertising copywriters have been quick to exploit. The fact remains, though, that some French cheeses are hard, and some English ones soft.

The essential arbitrariness between the written or spoken form of a word and its meaning is also illustrated by the story of the farmer leaning over his pigsty and remarking of its occupants: 'Ah, rightly is they called pigs!' Yet there is in fact no necessary connection between the smell and unpleasant feeding habits of the pig and the group of letters used to refer to it. This is borne out by listing the closely similar *big*, *dig*, *fig*, *jig*, *tig*, and *wig*, and possibly too by reflecting that, in Danish, *smukke pigges* means 'pretty girls'.

So we can see that the relationship between words and meanings is far from straightforward: when the words are short, the links are usually arbitrary. Moreover, we cannot, like Humpty Dumpty, simply make words mean anything we like, for they have conventionally accepted meanings, with new senses usually taking account of the ones that already exist. Of course, there are in English very many words whose meanings seem to be systematically connected to ways in which the words can be broken up. But of course these are not simple words: they are **complex words** such as *systematic* (a **derivative**) and *bookcase* (a **compound**). Both types will be dealt with in more detail in the next section, as a further step in exploring the complex relationships between words and meanings, words and words, and words and their meaningful components, which make up the subject of semantics.

Words, words, words

As soon as we embark on the study of semantics, we run up against the problem that we have to use words to talk about words, often in a technical sense rather different from the way they are used, rather more loosely, in ordinary conversation. The problem starts with the word 'word' itself! We can illustrate this by referring to a type of information about words that is commonly supplied in standard dictionaries. This is what we find if we refer to the entry for *write* in one well-known dictionary:

write ... (past '*wrote*'; past participle '*written*')

We do not need to understand the precise meaning of 'past participle' to realize that *wrote* and *written* are not additional items of vocabulary—as *writer*, say, or *write out* might be. On the contrary, they are modifications that we have to make to the verb *write* so that it will fit grammatically into various sentences. The use of '*wrote*', for example, normally requires some reference to the past, such as *I wrote to Bill yesterday*. By contrast, '*written*' can be combined with '*has*' or '*have*' to form the so-called perfect tense, like this: *I have already written to Bill*.

One way of capturing the difference is to say that there is one unchanging word—*write* (one constant **lexical item**) but that it takes on various 'forms' (has different **word-forms**) according to context. Notice finally that *write* has other forms, including '*writing*', but that as these are considered to be regular (i.e. of a kind that readers can work out for themselves) they are not spelt out in the dictionary.

I suggested above that, unlike '*wrote*' (say), *writer*, and *write out* were lexical items. They are indeed in various ways comparable to *write*. Many dictionaries will treat them in entries of their own, and they too, in parallel with *write*, have different, so-called **inflectional forms**, to suit the different contexts in which they function. Thus '*wrote out*' is the past tense form of *write out* and '*writers*' the 'plural form' of *writer*.

While we are clarifying the relationship between lexical items and their forms, we need to be aware of another distinction—the one between lexical and grammatical items. **Grammatical items**, also known as 'function words', form a relatively small part of the vocabulary. And they break down into a small number of classes—such as the 'demonstratives' *this*, *that*, *these*, *those*—whose members are typically few and seldom added to. Lexical items, by contrast, form a very large group, which is constantly expanding. And, of course, while grammatical items are few in number compared with lexical items, they occur much more frequently. This lopsidedness reflects the fact that while the function of lexical items is to express meanings, grammatical items provide the necessary cement holding phrases and sentences together.

When I referred earlier to the typical absence of any connection between the meanings of words and the words themselves, I limited this restriction to the shortest and simplest vocabulary items, such as *write*, *part*, *word*, *sound*, and *light*. As a general rule, the restriction does not apply to more complex items, and specifically to any which are made up of a simple word and an ending of some kind (as *writer* is), or of two simple words (as *write out* is). The first type is called a derived word (or derivative), the second a compound word (or more simply, compound).

As a glance at even a medium-sized dictionary will confirm, the compound words embodying (say) *air*, such as *airfare*, *airline*, *airmail*, and so on, greatly exceed in number the meanings of the simple word itself. If we add to the compounds the number of longer phrases incorporating *air* (for example, *on the air*, *airs and graces*, *walk on air*) we are left with the strong impression that meaning is often conveyed not so much by single simple words but by multi-word items (of various types). That is to say (in other words!) units of meaning do not always, perhaps do not usually, correspond to single-word units such as *air*, *write*, or *part*.

Multiple meaning

We have noted that units of meaning are not always confined to simple words, and that, as a rule, the forms of these words do not reliably indicate their meanings. The situation is further complicated by the fact that not only can similar meanings be expressed by words of quite different form (for example, *start* and *begin*) but words of identical form can often express quite different meanings. We are aware, too, that the meanings of words change to meet new needs, that the number of senses a lexical item may have varies considerably from one word to another, and that meanings constantly disappear, often because the objects and processes to which they refer have vanished or been replaced. As just one instance of the way existing words can be put to new uses, consider the items *server*, *crash*, *application*, *mouse*, and *document*, and the fresh meanings they have taken on in the field of computing. Or as an example of how words and their meanings can change in bewildering succession to reflect technical developments say, in sound recording and reproduction, note the following (partial) list: *gramophone record, long-playing record (LP), single, extended-play record (EP), CD, album*.

The name given to the existence of many meanings for a single word or phrase, and to the development of such meanings and their relatedness, is **polysemy**. The notion is often mentioned in the same breath as **homonymy** because traditionally much effort has been devoted to finding ways of distinguishing between them, both generally and in particular cases. When a given word (in the written language, a sequence of letters bounded on either side by a space) expresses two or more different but related meanings, we have polysemy. An example of a polysemous word is the verb *groom*, with its linked but separate senses:

(1) look after the coat of (a horse, dog, or other animal) by brushing and cleaning it;
(2) prepare or train (someone) for a particular purpose or activity.

If on the other hand the meanings are quite unrelated, as in the case of *light* ('not dark'), and *light* ('of little weight')—which incidentally are derived from different Old English words—we have homonymy: two separate vocabulary items which happen to share the same form.

Though polysemy and homonymy are often discussed together, the former is more widespread, and much more significant. Polysemy is typically the result of creativity and is crucial for the functioning of a language as an efficient signalling system. Imagine the loss of economy if every time we needed to convey a new idea we had to coin a new word. It is also true that the difference between homonymy and polysemy is not as clear-cut as people sometimes suppose, but more in the nature of a **gradation** or **scale**. So the various meanings of a particular word are more or less close to, or more or less distant from, each other. As an example of a word whose senses are closely related, take the noun *tour*, in the senses 'a spell spent in a country on duty', 'a sporting visit to various grounds', and 'an artistic visit to various centres'. Despite the fact that they are separately listed in several dictionaries, these meanings are hard to separate, as is underlined by the fact that we can say with reference to them all, 'They are on tour at the moment'.

Quite apart from their closeness or remoteness, what is the semantic nature of the connections between meanings in polysemous words? I suggested earlier that polysemy is typically the product of creativity. One type of creative process is metaphor. This can be illustrated by changes undergone by the word *caterpillar*. In the shift of meaning that has taken place here, aspects of the 'literal' meaning of the word—the worm-like movements of the segmented caterpillar—are transferred to another, the track of a tank or tractor, whose motion they are seen to resemble.

Meaningful relations

So far we have been considering the relationship between lexical items and their meanings. But words also relate to each other in various ways. When, for example, we are asked to explain the meaning of a word to somebody, we use other vocabulary items to do it—words which are related to it in meaning. One way of doing this, as we shall see in greater detail later on, is to use a short phrase incorporating a more general word than the one we wish to define. So, for example, we can say: 'a horn-beam is a tree ...'. And we can follow that up by adding detail which distinguishes the hornbeam from other trees: 'a decidu-ous tree with oval leaves and drooping flowers'. This of course is the approach commonly adopted in dictionaries. An alterna-tive is to provide a word with the same meaning as the one we wish to explain. So we might suggest *carry* as the equivalent of *bear* when what we have in mind is a waiter bearing a tray; *support* when *bear* is used in the context 'the pillars won't bear the weight of the arch'; and *endure* when we are referring to people who bear their afflictions bravely. Definition by means of **synonymy**, which is what we have here, is also a technique much favoured by dictionary-makers. Incidentally, the example makes a further point, that synonyms are not always the equivalents of a word as such. In this case, they relate not to the word *bear*, but *to bear* in each of three different senses.

Synonymy is probably the best known of a small number of relationships used by ordinary speakers of English to clarify the meanings of words. In semantics, though, the range of meaningful relations is much broader than those in general use and the various terms have benefited from precise definition. Ordinary users of the language can profit too, as they become aware of the many fine distinctions carried by a highly structured part of the vocabulary. Consider the term **antonymy**. Though quite widely used, this is often rather loosely defined as 'oppositeness'. But oppositeness can be understood in different senses. There is for instance the oppositeness of *lawyer* and *client*, or *teacher* and *pupil*. Here we are concerned with reciprocal professional roles, so that if I say 'I am your pupil', I imply 'You are my teacher' (and vice versa). Or there is the different oppositeness of *heavy* and *light*, or *rough* and *smooth*. Here the paired words are adjectives, not nouns, and they have the 'comparative' forms '*heavier*'/'*lighter*' and '*rougher*'/'*smoother*'. If we say 'John is heavier than Bill' we imply 'Bill is lighter than John' (and again vice versa).

So far, we have dealt with semantic relations that hold between one word and another. But such meaningful relations may be one-to-many (**hyponymy**). Consider, for instance, the item *dog* in relation to *collie*, *alsatian*, or *spaniel*. One way of accounting for the relatedness of *dog* to the other words is to say that its meaning is 'included' in theirs, since the characteristics of the species—its bark, the fact that it wags its tail when excited—are present in all three breeds. We find here an echo of the dictionary-type definition with which we began this section. There, it will be remembered, the item *hornbeam* was partly defined in relation to *tree*, whose meaning it includes.

The kind of one-to-many relationship we have just examined is one of the most important governing the structure of the vocabulary of English. It involves adjectives and verbs as well as nouns, since clearly the same kind of relationship holds between *red* and *crimson* (and between *cut off* and *chop off*) as between *dog* and *collie*.

Set sentences

We move now from meaningful relations between words to ways in which words combine with each other to form set expressions. Many of these are quite lengthy and complex, such as, for instance, *if you can't stand the heat get out of the kitchen* or *one man's meat is another man's poison* but, whether long or short, the key point to remember about them is that constant use in a particular form has made them more or less frozen, or fixed. We often refer to them in fact, as 'fixed phrases', and they form almost as important a part of the vocabulary as single words. Let us look at some of them in rather more detail. The examples we have just looked at are both complex—in fact they span complete sentences—but by far the largest group of phrases in English consists of expressions that are less than a complete sentence in length and indeed function as parts of sentences. Some familiar examples are the idioms *speak one's mind*, *close ranks*, *have an axe to grind*, and *by fair means or foul*.

We can all agree that **idioms** often present severe problems of meaning, a fact that is reflected in the familiar definition 'a group of words with a meaning that cannot be deduced from those of the individual words'. However, we need to extend that definition to account for two facts. The first is that idioms appear to vary in the extent to which their overall meaning is derived from those of the parts. Take for example *by fair means or foul*, where *fair means* is independently understandable. Then compare 'The means they used were perfectly fair', where the use of *foul* would strike us as rather dated.

The second qualification that has to be made concerns the figurative meaning of idioms. A considerable number have developed metaphorically from some existing, unproblematic, literal, or technical phrase. For example, in the case of an idiom such as *close ranks*, the whole of the (originally military) phrase has undergone a shift of meaning to become 'unite to defend common interests'. However, possibly in that case, and certainly in the case of *run into the buffers* and *go off the rails*, we retain some awareness of an earlier, literal meaning. The latter idiom is thus linked in our experience with its origins in railway usage.

I said earlier that phrases were typically fixed in form. However, just as some, as we have just seen, are not difficult to explain in terms of the meanings of their parts, so some are not entirely fixed in form. We can, for example, say *run* as well as *go off the rails*. Such examples suggest that phrases should be seen as spread along a **scale**, with the fully fixed and most 'opaque' in meaning at one end and the wholly free and most 'transparent' in meaning at the other.

Components of meaning

As we have already seen, accounting for the meanings of words in an orderly and illuminating way can take many forms. Our discussion of 'meaningful relations', for instance, focused on the words themselves and demonstrated how they are systematically related to each other. But we can also move 'inside' the word, and try to show how it is semantically structured, breaking the meaning down into more primitive elements.

We can illustrate one aspect of the semantic structure of words by going back to what was said earlier about **derivatives**—words such as *writer*, *reader*, or *booklet*, *twiglet*. Here, the smaller meaningful elements are actually visible, because taking *reader*, for example, we can detach the ending (more technically a **suffix**) -*er*, leaving the simple word *read* (the smallest meaningful unit that can occur alone, and for that reason also called a simple word). Suffixes and **prefixes**—similar units that are fixed to the *front* of a word—do not occur independently, but they do have meanings, so that -*er* means 'a person who (performs the action referred to by the verb)' while -*let* means 'a small (thing referred to by the noun)'.

Though simple words are potentially part of larger units— derivatives, compounds, or phrases—they can have as their equivalent or opposite any of the more complex types in particular cases. For example, *sad* has as its synonym *unhappy*, while *married* has as its opposite *unmarried* (which is synonymous with *single*). In the case of *sad* and *unhappy*, both words have the same semantic 'components' or 'features'. It is simply that the 'negative' feature is visible in one case, as the 'prefix' *un-*, but hidden in the other. And turning again to phrases, and their relationship to simple words, it is clear that *make certain* has the same components of meaning as *ensure*, and *by chance* the same semantic features as *accidentally*.

What are individual semantic features to be called? We referred above to a 'negative' feature, and clearly this could be applied to *single* and *unmarried*—without implying, of course, that the single state was something to be avoided! We should bear in mind, though, that 'negative', 'positive', and so on are not 'words' as we normally use the term, and as we have been discussing and illustrating them here. Rather, they are abstract terms, used in a special defining language to throw light on real words and the relationships between them. In describing a set of animal names, for instance, and showing precisely how they differ from each other, we might use the features 'animate' (i.e. 'living'), 'male', and 'adult'. This general approach, called **componential analysis**, often lends itself well to the description of **kinship groups** such as *father*, *mother*, *aunt*, etc. as well as to animal names. For instance, if we set up the contrastive components 'adult–non-adult' and 'male–female', as well as the distinction between 'human' and 'bovine', we can account for *man* as 'adult', 'male', 'human', and *bull* as 'adult', 'male', 'bovine'.

We need to be aware that not all words lend themselves to this kind of approach, with meanings broken down into contrasting features. Special symbols, and rules explaining how they are combined, are needed to tackle more complex groupings of words and meanings (see Chapter 6).

Summary

Having surveyed in this chapter a number of approaches to the description of words and their meanings, let us now go back over the main topics that have been touched on, highlighting as we proceed all the important technical terms. We began by noting that the shapes of the simplest words in English typically bore no relation to their meanings—that the word–meaning connection was essentially arbitrary. Moving on to discuss cases where meanings *could* be linked to the shapes of words, we found it useful to have as a general label lexical item, noting that this was more helpful than 'word' as it enabled us to clarify the distinction between the underlying, constant item (say, *write*), and the inflected forms by which it was realized in speech and writing ('*writes*', '*writing*', '*written*', '*wrote*'). We drew the further distinction between simple words, such as *write*, *part*, and *word*, derivatives, such as *writer* and *booklet*, and compounds, such as *town hall* and *dishwasher*. We then considered items with several meanings (i.e. polysemy), taking account of one of the different ways (i.e. metaphor) in which those senses developed and could be related. We went on to look at various kinds of systematic relationships *between* lexical items. These are known technically as sense relations. The most familiar are synonymy (compare *close/shut* and *prudence/caution*) and antonymy (compare *teacher/pupil* and *rough/smooth*). Also widespread, though less widely known, is hyponymy (a sense relation illustrated by *flower* in relation to *tulip* and *rose*, and *dog* in relation to *collie* and *spaniel*). We then moved on to consider fixed phrases, focusing especially on idioms. We saw that not all idioms are equally 'opaque', while many allow some adjustments to their form, as in *run* or *go off the rails*. Finally, we considered the internal semantic structure of lexical items, and in particular how they could be broken down into semantic features. One approach, known as componential analysis, and using such contrasted features as 'male' and 'female', has been used to analyse kinship relations, but other kinds of features are needed when describing items whose connections are not clear-cut.

As this summary shows, accounting for the forms and meanings of words in a revealing and systematic way can take various forms. But in the course of this chapter we have also been aware of an older tradition—that of the dictionary—and of its links with the modern, and more scientific subject of semantics. The practice in some dictionaries of defining words by means of their synonyms is only one instance of the linkage.

2

Word-formation

In the opening chapter we described in outline the processes by which the simplest words of English—the smallest independent units—can have **prefixes** and **suffixes** attached to them to form complex words, or derivatives. The change from *fill* to *refill* (or *pack* to *unpack*) illustrates prefixing, while the shift from *build* to *builder* (or *play* to *playful*) illustrates suffixing. Forming derivatives by the addition of those short elements can be contrasted with **conversion**, the process by which a lexical item is made a member of another word-class (part of speech) without the visible addition of a suffix or prefix. So we have *paper* (noun) and *paper* (verb), *yellow* (adjective) and *yellow* (verb). Then, finally, there is the possibility of one simple word being added to another to form a compound which, as shown here, may function as a noun, verb, adjective, or adverb: *team-mate*, *kick-start*, *roadworthy*, *level-headedly*. The building of new words by these various methods is known collectively as **word-formation**.

Lexicalization

The meaning of a derivative such as *builder* is arrived at by combining the meaning of the simple word (*build* in this case) and that of the suffix -*er* ('a person who does what is expressed by the verb'—here, 'a person who builds'). At first sight, the meanings of *builder* (or *baker*, say) seem to have been fully accounted for in the way I have just described. However, we normally use those words to refer to people who build or bake *for a living*. So, the meaning of the whole does not simply result from combining the meanings of the parts. What has happened is that, over time, the strong association between bakers, builders, and so on, and their paid occupations, has come to be reflected in the meanings of the words themselves. Derivatives whose meanings are extended with reference to their contexts in this way are said to be lexicalized.

Lexicalization, though, does not take place consistently in all the words referring to occupations—to limit the discussion simply to those. Take the case of *painter*. Here, two verb meanings have given rise to two nouns with corresponding senses:

(1) Bill has painted most of the houses round here. (Bill is a painter.)
(2) Mary has painted portraits of all her children. (Mary is a painter.)

As we can see, the noun *painter* can relate to either of the verb meanings. Yet there is an idiosyncratic difference. We could say of Mary that she was a painter even if her normal occupation was accountancy and she painted only as a hobby. The same could only be said of Bill if painting and decorating were his regular paid occupation.

Before we leave the theme of lexicalization altogether, let us turn to compounds, where, of course, the same phenomenon can be found. Take, for instance, *wheelchair* and *pushchair*. Both words refer to useful conveyances which have wheels and may be pushed. But wheelchairs are designed to carry invalids or elderly people while pushchairs are designed to carry small children. Yet there is nothing in the component words of *pushchair* to indicate its special function. Indeed, the bit of meaning 'for children' could have been assigned to *wheelchair*, had it not been for the fact that the latter, which appeared in 1700, had already laid claim to the invalid sense. When the smaller vehicles for children appeared in the early 1920s we must assume that the new meaning was assigned to a new term, *pushchair*, to prevent confusion.

Productivity

Before we begin to look at derivatives and compounds in greater detail, we should perhaps consider how much scope we have for creating new complex words of a particular type. One kind of restriction, sometimes referred to as **blocking**, is the exclusion of a derivative because a synonym already exists and may itself be a simple or complex word. It has been pointed out, for example, that despite the widespread use of the -*er* suffix there is no word *stealer* because of the prior existence of *thief* (or indeed *robber*). *Stealer* could, of course, be used by an individual on a given occasion (it is recorded in the *Oxford English Dictionary*, with the qualification that the object stolen must also be mentioned) but it would not become well-established unless it was used to refer to some new subclass of thieves.

Prefixes

Let us now turn to the three main types of derivation—by prefixing, by suffixing, and by conversion—and describe them in rather more detail. Prefixes make available to speakers a broad range of supplementary meanings that can be added to those already expressed by simple words alone. For example, the prefix *semi-* can be attached to words from various scientific fields, giving us *semiquaver*, *semicircle*, *semivowel*. Similarly, the addition of *poly-* ('many') produces *polytechnic*, *polyphonic*, and of particular importance in a book on semantics, *polysemy* (or 'multiple meaning'). By contrast, prefixes do not, by and large, play an important part in changing the grammatical classes of the words they are attached to.

A part-exception is the prefix *un-*. I say part-exception, because when you add *un-* to nouns such as *belief*, *truth*, and so on, with the meaning 'opposite of what the noun refers to' you get *unbelief* and *untruth*. No change of word-class there. But when the same prefix, this time with the meaning 'remove from what the noun refers to' (or, for short, 'remove from N') is attached to nouns such as *cage* or *seat*, *cage* becomes *uncage* and *seat* becomes *unseat*, and these derivatives are certainly not nouns, but verbs.

But these cases are the exception rather than the rule. For the most part, prefixes are concerned with the addition of a meaning to a word used within its existing class. Of course, it is possible for the prefix concerned to have two or more meanings. In the case of the prefix *sub-*, and when the definition is 'next in rank to the person N', we have one sense, which appears in *subagent*, *subdeacon*, *submaster*. But when the sense of *sub-* is 'division or part of the class N', we have in mind nouns such as *subclass*, *subregion*, and *subspecies*.

Suffixes

Whereas prefixes do not as a rule alter the class of the word to which they are attached, but do make available an assortment of additional meanings, suffixes—of which there are a good many more than prefixes—are typically class-changing and have rather less to say about meaning. In fact, it can be said of several suffixes that their *predominant* function is grammatical, and that they have little to do with meaning change. We can readily see, for example, how the ending -*ly* can be added to virtually any adjective, suggesting that its function is indeed reduced to signalling 'this word is now an adverb'. In a similar way -*ness* is very widely used to form abstract nouns, with the meaning 'the state of being X' (hence *happiness* and *kindness*). It is largely for this reason that adverbs in -*ly* and nouns in -*ness* (especially) are often not given separate entries in dictionaries but are included, without definitions, in the entries for the corresponding adjectives.

Change from one class to another is a characteristic feature of suffixing, and all the major parts of speech are involved—nouns, adjectives, adverbs, and verbs. So, for example, *organizer* and *government* (starting-point, verbs) and *happiness* and *elasticity* (starting-point, adjectives) have become nouns by the addition of -*er*, –*ment*, -*ness*, and -*ity*.

As we might expect, there are also differences of meaning *within* the classes of derivatives that are formed by such processes. Take, for instance, adjectives formed from nouns by the addition of the prefix -*less*. We have, among other examples, *childless*, *friendless*, *humourless*, all with the general meaning 'not having the person or thing N'. But we also have *cheerless*, *harmless*, and *painless*. Here, the meaning is not so much 'not having' as 'not giving or causing what is meant by the noun'. So a *harmless remark* means a remark that does not cause any harm.

We will sometimes find pairs of suffixes that are opposite in meaning. For example, the suffix *-less* of *cheerless*, *harmless*, and *painless* (just above) has the opposite *-ful*, giving *cheerful*, *harmful*, and *painful*. Note, though, that in the case of *painful*, it is the injury or limb which is painful, not the patient. (He or she may of course be painful in a different sense!) It is worth noting, too, that this particular contrast does not work for *childless* or *friendless*; we do not speak of a *childful* couple!

Conversion

Conversion, as we saw earlier, is a process by which a lexical item is made a member of another word-class without the addition of a suffix or prefix. It is unusually fruitful as a type of word-formation. However, the absence of prefixes or suffixes raises the question: how does the listener interpret—and how does the linguist explain—the meaning of the resulting noun, adjective, or verb? When we are dealing with derivatives such as *mountaineer* and *auctioneer*, the words can be explained by reference to the ending *-eer* ('skilled in working in/on X'; X here being mountains and auctions). But there is no such overt guidance in the case of *paper* in *John will paper the hall* or of *carpet* in *Jane will carpet the stairs* (the verbs in both cases being converted from the identically spelt nouns). The solution to the problem of interpretation is to ask what is characteristically done with wallpaper, carpet, plaster, or paint, the answer, of course, being 'we place it as a covering on a surface'.

Similarly with the verbs *belt*, *buckle*, *zip*, and *lace*. The characteristic use of belts, buckles, and so on, is to fasten, and the general definition of the verbs is therefore 'fasten a garment with X' (where X refers to the specific fastening).

The cases of conversion looked at so far have involved a change from one major class to another (noun to verb). But we also find examples of conversion *within* a class—say between intransitive and transitive verbs. Here we might be thinking of cases such as *the knives haven't polished up very well*, where the verb is 'intransitive', and *knives* is the subject, even though the polishing is intended to affect *them*. There is obviously a connection to a 'transitive' use, as in the sentence *we haven't been able to polish the knives up very well*, where *knives* is in its 'proper' place as the object of *polish*.

Compounds

Compounds are usually made up of two simple words, but either or both constituents may be further divided. So we have *windscreen wiper*, where the first element is a compound and *marriage breakdown*, where the second element is a compound, and *fast breeder nuclear reactor*, where both elements are compounds.

Despite the predominance of compounds which function as nouns (reflected in the above choice of examples) there are other important types, some adjectival and some verbal. All three will be touched on here. But staying with noun compounds for a moment, it is worth noting that the order in which the components occur, as for example in *haircut*, does not always match the order of elements in a paraphrase. Compare *he gave me a haircut* and *he cut my hair*. Several kinds of match, or mismatch, exist and three possibilities will be considered here.

It will be helpful to turn to Table 2.1, where the compounds are arranged in the first column and the sentence paraphrases in italics in the second. In the first two examples, *daybreak* and *nightfall*, we find that the order of words in the short sentences—*the day breaks* and *night falls*—is the same as the order of elements in the compound (*day* before *break* and *night* before *fall*). Here we have a match, and a highly productive type.

However, *haircut* and *handshake* display a contrastive relationship with the sentence paraphrase, as we have already seen.

	Compounds	Sentence Paraphrases
a	daybreak	*the day breaks* (subject + verb)
	nightfall	*night falls* (subject + verb)
b	haircut	*cut sb.'s hair* (verb + object)
	handshake	*shake sb.'s hand* (verb + object)
c	turncoat	*turn one's coat* (verb + object)
	cut-throat	*cut sb.'s throat* (verb + object)

TABLE 2.1 *Some noun-compound types*

In *cut somebody's hair* and *shake somebody's hand*, the order of the compound elements is reversed. (This type is moderately productive.)

Finally, consider the examples *turncoat* and *cut-throat*. Here the explanatory sentence has the same pattern as the one given for the two examples at (c) above. But in this case the ordering of compound elements is the same as in the paraphrase. Compare *killjoy*, *pickpocket*, and *breakneck* (as in *at breakneck speed*). This is no longer a fruitful pattern for compounds (the examples I have given are mostly dated), but it is more transparent, more self-explanatory, than the competing patterns. And as it happens, the pattern is still productive in French, where we find *tire-bouchon* 'corkscrew' (literally, 'pull cork') and *coupe-papier* 'paper-knife' (literally, 'cut paper'), among many others of the type.

Contrasting in internal structure with the various types of noun compound we have been looking at, are adjective compounds. In one type, of which *heartbreaking*, *life-restoring*, and *mind-blowing* are members, a noun element is present, followed by an *-ing* participle (sometimes called a 'present participle'). The meaning of the combinations is brought to the surface in the sentences *X breaks hearts*, *X restores lives*, and *X blows minds*.

Not every adjective compound, whether of this type or any other, will suggest a paraphrase that is as normal and natural-sounding as *X breaks (people's) hearts*, and this could well be a measure of how far the compound has petrified or become idiomatic. To see whether, or how far, this is true, consider examples such as *hard-boiled* (in the literal sense), *clean-shaven*, and *far-fetched*. Here, the constituents are an adjective (*hard*, *clean*) or an adverb (*far*) followed by an *-ed* participle (the 'past participle'). This gives us paraphrases such as *the egg was boiled hard*, but it is a different case with *clean-shaven*, where the paraphrase **he shaved himself clean* is bizarre alongside the entirely natural *he gave himself a close shave*. And even less acceptable is **it was fetched far*. (Asterisks indicate unacceptable sentences.) What this suggests is that *clean-shaven* and *far-fetched* are frozen in their compound forms. They are not structurally variable. We shall come across many such idiomatic compounds.

Finally, there are verb compounds. This is a curious category, since although the number of different sub-types is very small, one is quite remarkable in the way its compounds are formed. They are actually constructed by reversing a general principle governing derivation and compounding—the principle that says 'you end up with something more complex than you started with'.

Let us see again how that general principle is applied in a straightforward case of suffixing. Here we take a verb, add to it an *-or*, *-er*, or *-ar* suffix, and produce an 'agentive' noun. For the verbs *govern* and *act* the resulting nouns will be *governor* and *actor*. But what about *burgle* and *commentate*? The fact that these, too, have corresponding agentive nouns (*burglar* and *commentator*) suggests that the same process is involved as when *govern* becomes *governor* and *act* becomes *actor*. But this is not the case: *burgle* and *commentate* have been produced by *removing* something from *burglar* and *commentator*, a process known as **back-formation**.

Those were fairly straightforward cases of back-formation involving a simple word and a suffix. Let us turn to some rather more complex cases involving compounds, and see how these too can be turned into verbs. One very productive type of noun compound (of which *housekeeper* and *sightseer* are examples) is made up of a noun and an agentive noun ending in *-or*, *-ar*, or *-er*.

(3) housekeeper *X keeps   house* 'verb + object' noun + agentive noun

    sightseer   *X sees (the) sights* 'verb + object' noun + agentive noun

To change these to verb compounds we remove the agentive ending (with adjustment of spelling in the case of *seer*). This gives us *housekeep*, *sightsee*, both of which are verbs.

There is sometimes resistance from speakers to opening up the full range of tense forms of the verb *keep* (say) when it forms part of a verb compound produced by back-formation. We may accept *Jane housekeeps for us* (present tense) more readily than *Jane housekept for us* (past tense). And notice the parallel case of *babysit* (from *babysitter*). *I babysat for them* may still strike some speakers as more odd than *I'll babysit for them*. And oddest of all, perhaps, would be **I sat the baby for them*.

Winners and losers

Throughout this chapter we have been dealing with processes that are essentially open-ended. The rules provide for many more derivatives and compounds than actually exist at any one time. All the same, not every fresh coinage, useful and acceptable though it may at first appear, becomes firmly **established** in the language. Consider the case of *granny flat*. This type of apartment is typically attached to a house occupied by the grandparent's family, thus providing security while at the same time satisfying the elderly person's desire for a measure of independence. Does that give us a springboard for other compounds? Presumably a small house, built at the bottom of the garden to accommodate a grandparent, would be a *granny house*. And one could argue that, since neither term reflects the need that is doubtless felt by grand*fathers* for these admirable arrangements, we should also recognize *granddad flats* and *granddad houses*. All of these individual additions are perfectly justifiable, and there is ample precedent for this kind of expansion in other areas of the vocabulary (the 'lexicon'). The fact, though, is that apart from *granny flat* itself none of these items, if they have occurred at all, have cropped up often enough to be recorded in the *Oxford English Dictionary*. They have not caught on—they have simply not established themselves.

'Established' is a convenient term to apply to derivatives and compounds that have won acceptance by native speakers. Acceptance, of course, may be transitory: words may lose their appeal, or succumb to competition from later arrivals. Others live to a ripe old age. *Railway station*, first attested in 1838 at the dawn of the railway era, had to give some ground in the 1950s to *train station* (helpfully paralleled by *coach station* and *bus station*). Yet, half a century on, the older term is without serious rival, occurring over ten times as often as *train station* in spoken and printed texts.

3
Multiple meaning

In the last chapter we looked at the processes by which the simplest items of the vocabulary—words such as *play*, *team*, *start*—are made into derivatives by the addition of affixes, and into compounds by the bringing together of two simple words. Our aim was to explore the manifold processes of word-building, and for the most part we focused on the meanings which result from adding one 'literal' element to another. So, for instance, we were interested in *hardboiled* in relation to eggs, not in relation to people.

All the same, we could hardly not be aware that as well as being combinable with suffixes, the simple verb *play* (for instance) could also be used in several relatable meanings of its own (as in *play the piano*, *play football*, *play the stock-market*). The multiple meanings of a particular word—often developing from each other by creative processes such as metaphor—are known as its 'polysemy' and it is to polysemy in contrast with 'homonymy' that we now turn.

Polysemy and homonymy

Polysemy is often spoken of side by side with **homonymy** (two or more words with the same spelling, or sound, but quite different meanings) especially in traditional accounts of how meanings originate and multiply. A typical example of homonymy is *race*, with its two quite separate meanings: 'running' and 'nation' (or 'people'). These were once quite differcnt in written form as well (Old Norse *rās* and French *race*, respectively) but have converged over time under the influence of ordinary sound changes.

By contrast, we have polysemy when a particular word (in the written language, any sequence of letters bounded on either side by a space) has two or more separate though related meanings. Words with several meanings are, as a general rule, presented in dictionaries in a way that separates off the senses, and perhaps also shows the order in which they have emerged over time. Consider the entry for *mate* in one widely-used, historically-based dictionary:

> **mate**[1] ... **1** a friend or fellow worker. **2** Brit. colloq. a general form of address, esp. to another man. **3a** each of a pair, esp. of birds. **b** colloq. a partner in marriage.

Worth noting is the way numbers are used to mark off the meanings, and the introduction of letters, indicating that meanings (3a) and (b) are closer to each other than either is to any other 'major' sense. Worth noting, too, though almost unnoticeable, is the small number 1, tucked in above the **headword**: 'mate[1]'. This is an important detail, since it shows that there is (at least) a 'mate[2]', and that the two entries represent distinct words (the second being a term from the game of chess). They are, indeed, 'homonyms': two separate lexical items that happen to share the same form.

Though polysemy and homonymy are often spoken of together, polysemy is much more widespread. Homonymy may simply come about, as we have just seen in the case of *race*, through the chance merging of two different forms. And, indeed, in the dictionary we find the same thing: *gemate* 'messmate' gradually becoming 'mate[1]', and French *mat(er)* becoming 'mate[2]'. Polysemy, though, is typically the result of lexical creativity—and of course there is nothing to prevent polysemy developing within a homonym such as 'mate[1]', as has proved to be the case.

Polysemy has in fact a double value for speakers of a language. It provides scope *within* the word for new senses to emerge from those that already exist (compare a branch of the railway, a branch of the bank, and a branch of the subject). And it is economical, since it enables several related meanings to be expressed by a single form (actually, seven meanings in the case of 'mate[1]'), thus enabling communication to take place with great economy of means.

The origin and history of words (**etymology**) is certainly of interest to some students of language and users of dictionaries. It is not of much value, though, as a yardstick in settling disputes over whether, in one case or another, we are dealing with homonymy or polysemy. Interestingly, even if we were to insist that we rely simply on our knowledge of the language as it is today, we would often go astray. The lack of awareness that the ordinary native speaker typically has of word origins is shown by the case of *sole* and its meanings 'the underside of the foot or shoe' and 'a type of flatfish', respectively. The senses are historically linked, the second having developed from the first on the basis of similarity of shape. Nevertheless, many native speakers will think they are unconnected, an assumption that is no doubt encouraged by dictionaries which treat the items as separate entries.

The difficulty that native speakers may have in recognizing related meanings—or their absence—is also illustrated by the two current senses of the French noun *grève*: (1) a beach or shoreline and (2) a strike (on the part of workers). These may seem quite unrelated, yet the second meaning sprang historically from the first. Till about the middle of the nineteenth century, men looking for work would foregather in an open space (Place de Grève) adjoining the river Seine. (English *gravel* is a diminutive of *grave*, in one meaning, which is in turn related to *grève*.) The men would be said to *faire grève*, or *être en grève*. Then, later, the phrase *faire grève* came to mean the opposite: to stop work as a means of pressing for an increase in wages.

An example such as *grève* supports the idea, whether we are ordinary speakers or trained linguists, that the difference between homonymy and polysemy is often difficult to determine, and certainly not clear-cut. Then among all the individual cases of polysemy, some meanings are close together, while others are more remote. What we need is a set of procedures to help us make up our minds in particular cases, and it is to devising this that we now turn our attention.

Testing for meanings

The central problem we need to tackle is precisely how we identify polysemy in particular cases and how we distinguish meanings that are close together from those that are far apart. Being able to capture these fine differences should help us to throw light on how meanings develop (or cease to develop) over time. For all of this we need reliable means of backing up the claims we make. We need suitable tests; and we need to know whether we should take account of more than one. The following examples illustrate the kind of problem that crops up:

(1) The paper stuck to the wall.
(2) The committee stuck to its agreed agenda.

What test or tests can we apply in this case to determine whether the two uses of *stick to* correspond to two meanings? A test which shows whether the verb can be made 'passive' in either or both cases seems to work well. A change to the passive is possible in the second example (*the agreed agenda was stuck to*) but not in the first (*the wall was stuck to*), thus suggesting that the verb in the two examples has separate senses.

But the passive test, like any other single criterion, can only take us so far. It is one measure of the separateness of the two uses, but does not tell us if the senses are nonetheless related (polysemy) or quite distinct (homonymy). Helpfully, there is evidence at hand from another test, in which we try to replace the verb in each example by a synonym. Here the test suggests that the meanings are related, since *adhered to* can replace *stuck to* in both examples. So here we have polysemy: relatedness as well as difference.

This simple procedure has brought to light polysemy in a single case. If we were able, though, to deploy a battery of tests we would be in a position to show that polysemous words differ quite widely according to how closely or distantly their meanings are related. (In fact showing *degrees* of similarity or difference is one of the key purposes served by using a wide range of criteria.)

As we have suggested, however, analysing a number of polysemous words in this way will not only reveal degrees of relatedness. It should also throw light on the evolution of meaning over time, the assumption being that the more two or more meanings diverge, the more they will tend to attract their own opposites and synonyms, and as we have just seen, grammatical patterns. This claim is borne out by the way meanings have developed in the adjective *responsible*, and specifically the two senses 'having the job or duty of looking after someone or something' and 'dependable or trustworthy'. In the first sense, but not in the second, the adjective is synonymous with *answerable* (often accompanied by *to someone*, *for something*). In the second meaning, but not in the first, the adjective has the opposite *irresponsible*. The indications, then, are that the meanings have moved away from each other.

For an example of the opposite phenomenon of meanings remaining relatively close to each other, we turn to the noun *tour*. Here is an item whose senses have, on the whole, been resistant to forming new derivatives (such as *tourist* from *tour*) and compounds (such as *tour-operator* from *tour* and *operator*). In fact, of the following set of meanings, (a) to (e), only the first is associated with an appreciable spread of complex words:

(3) a	**tour** (holidays)	tour (*v*), tourism, tourist; tour-operator, package tour; go on/make a tour (of the Alps)
b	**tour** (visit, inspection)	tour (*v*), go on/make a tour (of the factory)
c	**tour** (military)	tour (*v*), go on/be on tour
d	**tour** (artistic)	tour (*v*), go on/be on tour
e	**tour** (sporting)	tour (*v*), tourist go on/be on tour

Here, indeed, *tour* (a) has thrown up, as derivatives, *tourist* and *tourism*, and as compounds, *tour-operator* and *package tour*. There are also *tourists* in a sporting sense, it is true, but otherwise the military, artistic, and sporting meanings, though separable from (a) and (b), are difficult to set apart from each other. Note that in referring to all three we can say *he's on tour at the moment*. To sum up, we may be dealing here with recurrent uses that are not yet fully established as separate meanings.

Specialization of meaning

We have seen that the meanings of polysemous words may diverge, as in the case of *responsible*, or be close together, as in the case of *tour*. The question we then have to answer is: by what processes were those meanings created in the first place? One widespread and important mechanism is **specialization of meaning**. It is illustrated by developments in one of the chief meanings of the verb *smoke* ('inhale and exhale the smoke of tobacco or a drug'). In this general sense, *smoke* occurs with a readily identifiable range of object nouns: *cigarette*, *cigar*, *pipe* (to say nothing of *hash* and *hemp*), and in various tense forms. There is, however, a related meaning, normally excluding the use of an object but calling for the addition of *heavily*. So we have *she smokes heavily*, *they smoked heavily*, and so on. This prompts two reflections. The first is that the meaning of *smoke* in such cases is restricted in reference, *heavy smokers* being a subclass of *smokers* in general. And the sense is *specialized*, since the focus is now on the habitual (and possibly health-threatening) character of smoking rather than the activity itself. The health-conscious aspect of the specialized sense is reflected in a well-established detail of patterning. Though the British National Corpus (BNC) certainly contains examples of *she/they smoke(s) heavily* (six examples in fact), they are few compared with instances of the noun phrases *heavy smoker(s)* and *heavy smoking*, which amount to fifty-seven. Here is another shift of emphasis, to a social category and activity as a focus of public and official concern. Alongside smoking, alcohol and especially over-consumption of it, are common subjects of concern for the health conscious, so it is not surprising that, in parallel with the *smoke* patterns, we have *he/she drinks heavily*, *heavy drinker*, and *heavy drinking*.

Metaphor

The familiarity and importance of **metaphor** as a means of creating new senses make it a vital topic for discussion. A number of metaphors have already appeared as examples in this chapter. There was the case of *sole* (from Latin *solea*). Historically, *solea*, which first referred to the underneath of the foot, came to be applied to the flatfish, on the grounds of similarity of shape. So the meanings are not separate but linked. There is also a *caterpillar* metaphor, one which attributes the characteristics of the larva, specifically its segmented body and movements that follow the contours of the ground, to the track of a tank or tractor.

From these examples we can derive a pattern or structure which is common to many individual metaphors. There is first the so-called **tenor**, the starting-point of the metaphor (the 'flat-fish' meaning in the case of *sole*). Then there is the **vehicle**, the image chosen to represent, or stand for, the tenor (the caterpillar meaning in the second case). Lastly, there is the **ground** of the metaphor, the perceived similarity between tenor and vehicle which provides the basis for the comparison (shape in the case of *sole*, shape and movement in the case of *caterpillar*).

As well as illustrating the structural elements of the metaphor, those examples serve as a reminder that the vocabulary of English contains metaphors in various stages of 'moribundity' (or terminal decline). We have already suggested that few native speakers will be aware of the relatedness of the *sole* (or *grève*) meanings. Perhaps the source of the *caterpillar* comparison is more easily evoked. Here too, of course, is a clear connection with the idea, developed earlier, of relative 'distance' between meanings.

The case of *shuttle* raises rather a different point—the influence of technology on the emergence and disappearance of meanings. Its metaphorical development goes along familiar lines. Similarities are perceived between the movements of a weaver's bobbin (a cylinder holding thread) 'moving backwards and forwards regularly' and aircraft, trains, buses, and (increasingly) spacecraft providing a constant to-and-fro service. Thus was the metaphor born. But we know from cases already considered that if a metaphor is used sufficiently often in a particular sense, it loses the power to shock or surprise, and speakers (and dictionary-makers) 'encode' the metaphorical meaning as one of the standard senses of the word.

The additional factor in this case is that, through technological development, the earlier, industrial meaning has receded to such an extent in the experience of speakers (and the metaphorical 'transport' senses have come so far to the fore) that the word in its earlier sense is very seldom used. Evidence for this comes from the BNC and the fact that, influenced by the relative frequencies of the meanings in the BNC, many dictionaries put the transport senses first, despite their later appearance in the language.

Classes of metaphors

We have looked at a number of metaphors, more or less separately, to explain what metaphors are, as distinct from other figures of speech, and how they are structured. But what may also strike the reader, as examples of metaphors accumulate, is that certain kinds of relationship existing between literal and figurative meanings recur, suggesting the setting-up of a number of major categories or classes. The caterpillar metaphor, as you will have noticed, belongs to a class that attributes animate features to an inanimate object. The sole metaphor ('fish' and 'human foot') attributes characteristics of human beings to non-human creatures. Various classes of linkage between literal and figurative metaphors have been identified, and we can consider some of them here (with **italics** highlighting the metaphors).

- We have seen examples of the 'concretive' metaphor, which attributes concreteness or physical existence to an abstraction: *stock-market* crash and *computer system* crash belong here, as does *the* collapse *of Lehman Brothers*.
- There are also 'animistic' metaphors, which attribute animate characteristics to an inanimate object. The caterpillar *track* metaphor clearly fits here, as do *the* wing *of an aircraft* and *the* belly *of a ship*.
- Finally, we have the 'humanizing' (or 'anthropomorphic') metaphor, which attributes characteristics of humans to non-human objects: we talk of *the* brow *of the hill*, *the* eye *of a needle*, *the* heart *of the matter*, *the* neck *of a bottle*.

Metonymy

Metaphor, the creative process we have been considering, and **metonymy**, the one we shall go on to talk about, can both be covered by the dictionary definition 'a figure of speech that consists in using the name of one thing for the name of something else with which it is associated'. This is broad enough to capture both processes for deriving one word-meaning from another. But it can also be adapted to refer to one or the other. If we replace 'with which it is associated' by 'which it *resembles* in some respect' (so, *caterpillar* for *track*, *shuttle* for *train*) we define metaphor.

And if we replace 'with which it is associated' by 'with which it is connected in some respect' (so, *crown* for *monarch*, *sail* for *ship*), we define metonymy.

It has been suggested that metonymy is intrinsically less interesting than metaphor since it does not discover new connections between words but brings into play words that are already related (as *crown* is to *monarch*, for instance). All the same, metonymy is one of the chief ways in which multiple meaning arises, and is of value in enabling a speaker or writer to achieve economy and pithiness of expression. And, as we shall see, many instances of metonymy are highly creative. For these various reasons, it deserves further exploration.

Consider the word *village*, used in its 'literal' sense to refer to a small, inhabited location. That meaning is conveyed by the example *the village is crossed by a major road*. But what about this example: *the village has welcomed the construction of a bypass*? *Village* here can only mean 'the people of the village'. What has happened is that the literal sense of *village* has been extended to include *human* features alongside the original reference to *location*. And returning for a moment to the point about economy of expression, note that the extended meaning of *village* can be conveyed by simple reuse of the same noun.

Other specific 'rules' are allowed for within the same general principle. One such rule allows us to use a word denoting such-and-such a composer or author with the meaning 'the works of such-and-such a composer or author'. So we have *I love early Bach* (meaning 'I love the early works of Bach'). Another rule permits us to use a word referring to a particular place in the sense 'the event that occurred in that place'. That can be illustrated by *It was two years after the Wall* (meaning 'It was two years after the Berlin Wall was torn down'). Application of the rule, incidentally, by which the name of a place implies that of its occupant(s) may have particular effects when the place is Number 10 or the White House. Does it allow reporters (say) to refer to all of the powerful occupants without putting themselves at risk by mentioning any of them by name?

New applications of such rules are constantly occurring. One application may be emerging in a current use of *ball* by rugby players and commentators. The noun *ball* in the sense 'a single delivery of the ball' is long established, and is a clear case of metonymy. But there is evidence of an interesting new meaning in the example *a strong scrum providing the backs with some good ball*, where *ball* is a so-called 'mass' noun that can be glossed as 'a good supply of deliveries of the ball'. Here the principle being put to work is again metonymy, except that here we are drawing on the 'delivery' sense of *ball* and not directly on the original concrete meaning. Here we are reporting the arrival of a new sense. The rule of which it is an example, though, has been applied on many earlier occasions.

Creativity and slang

Occasionally, the processes which give rise to metonymy operate in combination with rules of another type to provide striking and often humorous results. This is particularly the case with **slang**, a special vocabulary whose chief purpose is to identify and encourage a sense of community in members of a professional, service, or social subgroup, and which for this purpose employs verbal wit and inventiveness. Consider, in the Royal Navy, the officer responsible for launching torpedoes at enemy ships. His nickname is *torps*. This is an abbreviation of *torpedo officer*, though with the –s doing duty as a 'familiarity' ending (also found in sporting nicknames: *Morgs*, from Morgan and *Daws*, from Dawson), and with *officer* concealed, so as to make *torps* refer to the weapon as well as the man. The metonymy is then: *torps* is 'the name of the weapon applied to the person associated with the weapon'.

The nickname *guns*, for *gunnery officer*, and *flags*, for *flag lieutenant*, follow the same path as *torps*. The nicknames *sparks* and *chips*, however, take a different path, more complex and more humorous. Here the familiarity endings are in place, but *sparks* and *chips* are clearly not a description of duties performed by a wireless operator or a ship's carpenter. They are, if anything, the by-products of their duties! So, it is the sparks and chips humorously associated with radio messages and carpentry which are attributed, by metonymy, to the crew-members concerned, and which give them their memorable nicknames.

4

Meaningful relations

Word-formation, as we saw in Chapter 2, is concerned with the ways in which simple words combine with endings (or with each other) to form derivatives and compounds. Words, prefixes, and suffixes are like building blocks, with a variety of rules determining which piece can combine with which, and with what meaningful results. In this chapter, by contrast, we are concerned not with the construction of new words from existing parts but with the semantic *relationships* which words enter into with each other. As we shall see, these relationships may involve pairs of words (for example, *married/single*; *slow/fast*; *husband/wife*; *arrive/depart*). But as well as forming pairs (that is, entering into 'binary' relations), words may come together in more complex groupings: *thrush, sparrow, finch*; *lieutenant, captain, major*; *spring, summer, autumn, winter*. We shall begin by considering one example of a pair and one of a complex grouping, noting particular features but also taking account of stylistic factors, for instance, the difference between formal and informal items and pairs and the interaction between semantic relations on the one hand and multiple meaning (polysemy) on the other.

Pairs and groupings: synonymy

The binary relationship which is probably best known, at least by name, is **synonymy**, or sameness of meaning, illustrated by the adverbs *scarcely* and *hardly*. Also synonymous, on the face of it, are the verbs *begin* and *start* and the adjectives *quick*, *fast*, and *rapid*. We shall see, though, that to say two words 'have the same meaning' gives us a picture of synonymy which is far from complete. One problem is that two words, though equivalent in meaning, may differ in 'formality'. So, *rapid* and *swift* are more formal in style than either *quick* or *fast* (compare *a rapid response* and *a quick response*). The same kind of stylistic difference can be seen in the choice of *commence* in the first of the following examples and *kick off* in the other:

(1) When did the meeting commence? (formal)
(2) What time did the meeting kick off? (informal)

Another factor that cannot be overlooked when giving a proper account of synonymy (and of various kinds of oppositeness, too) is the part played by the multiple meaning (or polysemy) of the words we are dealing with. Consider again the two adverbs *scarcely* and *hardly*. *Scarcely*, as it happens, has meanings which are closely matched by those of *hardly*, as we can see from these examples:

(3) Scarcely/hardly had I taken my coat off when the post arrived.
(4) We've scarcely/hardly seen a customer all morning.

Also noticeable is that, in each case, the synonyms appear in the same grammatical patterns. We notice especially that for the meaning in Example (3), the adverbs come first, and that the order of subject and verb is reversed (*had I*). It seems reasonable, then, to claim that the words are synonymous *as wholes*, and not simply in relation to some of their senses. Such cases, though, especially where the non-technical, 'general' vocabulary of English is concerned, are extremely rare. What we generally find is that one or more senses of word A are the same as one or more senses of word B, without, however, all the senses providing a perfect match. This more usual pattern is illustrated by the nouns *goal* and *aim*. While the words have one meaning in common ('a desired result or outcome') *goal* has the familiar sporting senses which are not shared with *aim*; furthermore *aim* has the sense 'pointing a weapon or missile at a target' which is not shared with *goal*. As I have suggested, we shall find the same kind of partial mismatch cropping up when later on we look at various kinds of oppositeness.

Pairs and groupings: ranks

As one example of a grouping of words and of the relationships it enters into, we can consider **rank**. Ranking is concerned with the way in which positions on a seniority ladder (say in the armed forces or civil service) are described relative to each other. The key relationship is 'immediately above or below'. So we say (referring to military ranks) that *sergeant* is 'immediately above' *corporal* and 'immediately below' *colour-sergeant*.

Notice, by the way, that the 'slang' forms of address *corp*, *sarge*, and *colour* are related to each other in the same way as their formal equivalents. Also that polysemy has a part to play in a fuller description of *sergeant*. A police sergeant belongs to a different organization, with different duties, from his or her military namesake, so that the word *sergeant* is polysemous. But in the British police force, a sergeant ranks immediately below an inspector, so that the two meanings of *sergeant* can also be stated in terms of positions on different scales of rank.

In the army, at least, sergeants are part of a more elaborate structure. As well as being above their juniors and below their seniors, sergeants (together with colour-sergeants) are also 'senior non-commissioned officers' ('senior NCOs'), while corporals and lance-corporals are 'junior NCOs'. Senior to all NCOs are the sergeant majors—by tradition seen as remote and awesome figures, and in consequence the butt of much regimental humour. The most exalted of these, the regimental sergeant major (or RSM), stands at the pinnacle of all those in a regiment who have no 'commissions', that is, who are not officers. Those who *do* have commissions form a special and distinct group, but as individuals they too are ranked one above the other, captains above lieutenants, majors above captains. And forming the base of the great overall structure are the 'other ranks'—the privates who have yet to earn a single badge or sew on a single stripe.

Binary contrasts: antonyms

In traditional treatments of semantics, the term **antonymy** was often used, rather imprecisely, to refer to 'oppositeness'. One of the strengths of modern semantics has been to break down this traditional and rather loosely defined notion into three more pre-cisely delineated categories: 'complementarity', 'converseness', and (in a strict sense) 'antonymy'. Here, we will focus on each of these relationships in turn, beginning with antonymy in the narrow and exact meaning.

Examples of antonyms are *long/short*; *fast/slow*; *precise/imprecise*. In these and other examples of the type, we have two fully 'gradable' adjectives, that is, adjectives with a 'comparative' and a 'superlative' form: *'faster'*, *'fastest'*; *'more precise'*, *'most precise'*, and so on. Of course, the actual length, speed, degree of precision, and so on, will vary from one type of object or event to another. A long pencil may be rather short in absolute terms, and a short conflict, rather long.

Another key feature of antonymous adjectives is that they can be regarded as 'moving' in opposite directions along a particular scale—in the following case a scale of speed—when modified by *very*, *fairly*, etc.

(5) very fast ← fairly fast ___ fairly slow → very slow

There are important subclasses of antonyms within the general class. Let me mention just one, the so-called 'polar' antonyms. Here, the property along the scale has to do with measurement in terms of exact height (whether of a building or a person), age, and so on, and thus of metres, feet, and years. Typical pairs are *high/low*; *tall/short*; *old/young* (but not *rough/smooth*; *fat/thin*).

Let us deal with the 'exact measurement' aspect first. Using the adjective *high*, we can say *the wall is six feet high* (compare *the wall is six feet in height*), but not **the wall is three feet low*. There are the same possibilities and restrictions with *tall* and *short*: *Bill is six feet tall*, but not **Bill is four feet short*. Notice, incidentally, that in the case of *non*-polar *fat* and *thin*, neither adjective can combine with an exact measurement: **Fred is sixteen stone fat* is as unacceptable as **Fred is twelve stone thin*.

Then there is the matter of how polar adjectives behave in questions introduced by *how*. One member of a pair such as *old/young* is more flexible in the sense that you can form a question *How old is she?* which, with emphasis on *old*, makes no assumptions concerning the person's age. (Compare *What is her age?* which has the same meaning.) *How young is she?* though, with emphasis on *how*, implies that she is young, and is aimed at clarifying what point she has reached in this part of her life.

Binary contrasts: complementaries

As an example of another two-word relationship take the contrast between *married* and *single*. To understand this kind of oppositeness, called **complementarity**, and this particular example, it helps to imagine a world of 'marriageable adults', divided into two mutually exclusive groups, married and single, so that it is true to say: *If Jane isn't single, she must be married.* (And, *If John isn't married he must be single.*) This is fine as far as it goes, but there is an inherent untidiness, too, and to capture it we need to add to the analysis that being divorced implies prior marriage, and that divorced people are either single or remarried.

Complementarity is an important type of contrast that usually involves adjectives, though not 'gradability' (that is, the adjectives concerned do not have comparative and superlative forms, such as *fast, faster, fastest* or *horrible, more horrible, most horrible*). As with other types of oppositeness, complementaries may be entirely unrelated in form, as in the case of *dead/alive*, or the contrast in meaning may be signalled by a prefix or suffix, as with *attached/unattached*. With other complementaries, there may be alternation between a word with a prefix or suffix and one without either, as in the case of *married, unmarried/single*.

The examples I have chosen may have given the impression that the difference between antonymy and complementarity is always clear-cut. That this is not always the case, though, is made clear by the oppositeness of *black* and *white* in various meanings. In a game of chess we have black pieces and white pieces—a clear case of complementarity, one would think, as the game of chess divides its pieces into two mutually exclusive sets. But consider *black* and *white* as applied to coffee drunk, say, after a meal. Since a cup of coffee may, on different occasions, need to contain more or less milk, it is natural for speakers to say *I'd like mine a little more white* or *I like mine almost black*, introducing degrees of blackness or whiteness along a scale, and thus antonymy. And, of course, since *black* and *white* each have two meanings here, one involving gradability and one not, polysemy is involved.

Binary contrasts: converses

When we say that *John is Mary's husband* we of course imply that *Mary is John's wife*. The linked sentences illustrate a reciprocal type of oppositeness, known as **converseness**, which is also found in the linked pair *Fred is Jane's uncle* and *Jane is Fred's niece*.

In each of these examples of converseness there are two participants (*John* and *Mary*; *Fred* and *Jane*) and two 'converses' (*husband* and *wife*; *uncle* and *niece*). And here, too, we are involved with noun converses that reflect a personal or family relationship. However, converseness is also common in parts of the lexicon concerned with reciprocal social roles, for example, *doctor/patient, lawyer/client, tutor/student*. This calls for a similar pattern to the one already shown:

(6) *Mary is Emma's doctor* implies *Emma is Mary's patient*.

There is a curious lopsidedness, known as 'markedness', in several of the converses that refer to social roles. The pair *doctor* and *patient*, for instance, have a 'relational' meaning, one that has to do with their professional interaction. But while *patient* simply has the relational sense (it means 'someone who consults and is treated by a doctor', and is 'marked') being a doctor is more than the sum of his or her professional links with patients, and is 'unmarked'. A doctor has a professional status and title deriving from his or her lengthy training which make sense of the question and answer *'What do you do?' 'I'm a doctor.'* (Compare *'What do you do?' 'I'm a patient.'*) In the case of *tutor* and *student*, on the other hand, a more even balance is struck. As well as being defined in terms of his or her relationship to a tutor, a student has an independent status, as is borne out by *'What do you do?' 'I'm a student.'*

Groupings: hyponymy

The relationship known as **hyponymy** is brought into play when we say *Max is a collie* implies *Max is a dog*, for example, but then go on to say, contrastively, *Max is a collie* is not implied by

Max is a dog. In less technical language, saying that Max is a dog does not mean saying that he is a collie. (He might equally well be a terrier or a spaniel.)

Here we have a general word (*dog*) and more specific words or phrases (*collie*, *terrier*, *spaniel*). In semantics the former is referred to as the **superordinate** and the latter as 'hyponyms'. There are, of course, many different general and specific words in the lexicon standing in the relationship of superordinate to hyponym. Bird and animal names are obvious cases, as are the names of flowers and vegetables. Consider *flower* (superordinate) in relation to *daffodil*, *rose*, and *tulip* (hyponyms). And note, too, *root vegetable*, *green vegetable* ('greens'), *pulse* and *tuber*, all of which are hyponyms of the superordinate *vegetable*.

Then, as this last set of items may also suggest, a description can often be extended to form a hierarchy with several levels of specificity. We have seen that *pulse* and *tuber* are **co-hyponyms** (that is, joint hyponyms) of *vegetable*, but equally *bean* and *pea* are co-hyponyms of *pulse*, and *potato* and *cassava* of *tuber*. (And, in the same way, *cabbage* is a hyponym of *green vegetable*, and *parsnip* a hyponym of *root*.) A clearer impression of the various relationships in the branching hierarchy (which is however far from complete) can perhaps be conveyed by means of a **tree diagram** (Figure 4.1 below):

Superordinate–hyponym relationships exist between lexical items of all the major word-classes, so between adjectives, verbs, and adverbs as well as nouns. As regards adjectives, we can say that *it is a crimson flower* implies *it is a red flower*, where *crimson* is the hyponym. In the case of verbs, we can say *he's a man*

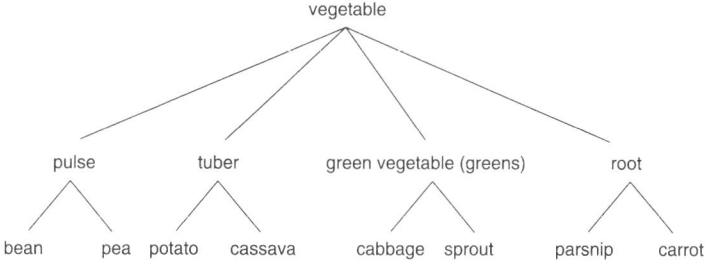

FIGURE 4.1 *Branching hierarchy: vegetables*

who chops down trees implies *he's a man who cuts down trees*, where *chop down* is the hyponym. And with regard to adverbs, we can say *they applauded thunderously* implies *they applauded noisily*, where *thunderously* is the hyponym.

I suggested earlier, referring to 'co-hyponyms' in the complex vegetable hierarchy that was being built up, that the relationship between the various words at the same level of specificity was as significant as the 'downward' relationship between superordinate and hyponym. Items such as *collie, spaniel,* and *alsatian* are alike in being hyponyms of the same superordinate, *dog*, since it is possible to say that *this is a spaniel* implies *this is a dog*. Equally, *this is an alsatian* implies *this is a dog*. At the same time, these co-hyponyms are mutually exclusive, since *this is a spaniel* implies *this is not an alsatian, not a collie*.

In very many hierarchies, including the vegetable hierarchy, there are differences between co-hyponyms according to level of formality or restriction to particular types of user. Looking back at the 'vegetable' diagram, we notice that among the co-hyponyms of *vegetable, greens* is the more informal equivalent of *green vegetable*, while *tuber* is a term more likely to be used by gardeners and botanists than the ordinary native speaker. With the growth of health food stores, on the other hand, and thanks to the popularity of dried peas and beans, *pulse* has become a more familiar term. Among the most specific items, almost all are in general use in Britain, except for *cassava* (and *yam*), staple elements in many Afro-Caribbean diets, though gaining wider popularity elsewhere.

Sometimes the grouping of a number of key terms in another language makes us see all or part of the corresponding area of the English lexicon in a different light. Consider, for example, the terms used in French to refer to major types of trees—words or phrases which reflect such properties as the shedding of leaves (or needles) in autumn. These major types seem to lend themselves to analysis in terms of superordinates and (co-)hyponyms, as in Figure 4.2 below:

This layout—appropriately enough, a tree diagram—captures the main distinctions. Chief among these, as it has to do with the shedding or retention of leaves or needles, is the contrast between the picturesquely named *arbre à feuilles persistantes* ('evergreen') and the archaic *arbre à feuilles caduques* ('deciduous tree'; the

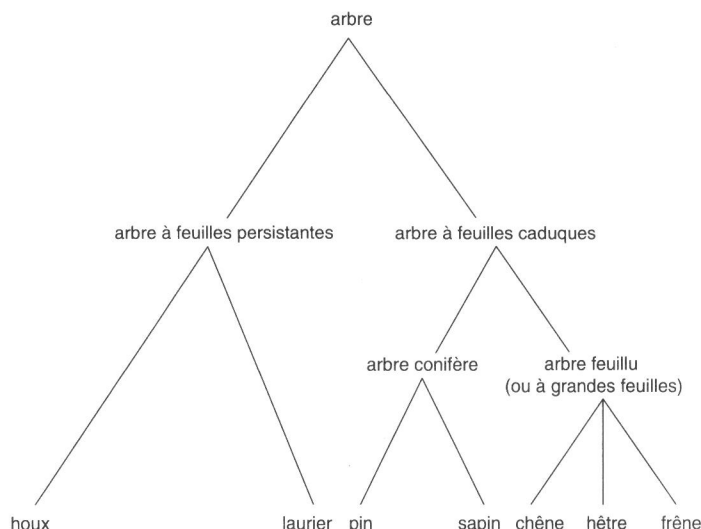

FIGURE 4.2 *Major tree types in French*

original meaning of *caduc, -que* being 'nearing its end and about to fall'). These two key terms are complementaries, and also co-hyponyms of *arbre*. On the next level down we have the contrast (also one of complementarity) between the *arbre conifère* ('coni-fer') and the *arbre feuillu* (also called *arbre à grandes feuilles*, or 'broadleaved tree'). This distinction is important, too, because it captures the difference between deciduous trees which shed needles and those which shed leaves. Then finally, we move to a sample of actual tree names: *houx* (holly), *laurier* (laurel), *pin* (pine), *sapin* (fir), *chêne* (oak), *hêtre* (beech), *frêne* (ash).

You might expect to find a scientific or semi-scientific field such as this reflected more or less point for point in an English categorization of tree types. This is broadly what happens. The well-known terms *evergreen* and *deciduous* mark the same con-trast as the French terms do at the top level of the analysis. The contrast between the two diagrams lies on the next level, and it boils down to a difference in how the ordinary French speaker reacts to *arbre feuillu* (or *arbre à grandes feuilles*) and the ordin-ary English person to *broadleaved tree*. For French speakers, *arbre feuillu* is part of everyday usage, more or less on the same footing as *à feuilles caduques*, and generally perceived as non-scientific. It has been in the language since the 1870s. *Broadleaved tree*, though, will certainly not be as familiar to English speakers as *deciduous* or *evergreen* since it is still largely a term for specialists (two-thirds of the fifty-odd appearances of the word in the BNC are in texts devoted to rural development).

Perhaps the word deserves wider currency. As well as giving the 'leaves' end of the 'leaves–needles' contrast a lexical presence, it might serve to sharpen perceptions that, just as softwood has one collective source (conifers), so hardwood has another (broadleaved trees). In the meantime, the space which *broadleaved tree* occupies for specialists is for many, perhaps most, ordinary English speakers a 'lexical gap'—a place in the organization of the lexicon where existing contrasts and dependencies, as in this case, suggest that a word should be present but where none exists.

Groupings: non-branching hierarchies

The groupings of which *vegetable* and *dog* (and *arbre*) are the superordinates are **branching hierarchies**. They branch in the sense that co-hyponyms at the lowest level (say, *pea*, *bean*) lead us back to a common point (at *pulse*), while *pulse* with co-hyponyms of its own (say, *tuber*, *root*) bring us to the upper meeting point of the branching, i.e. the overall superordinate.

Many ordered groupings in the lexicon, though, are **non-branching**. They are linear arrangements of words (or words in particular meanings) with an unchangeable sequence and a first and last item. This is true of the various recognized stages in a human life (though, notice, it would be difficult to establish exact boundaries between the stages):

(7) babyhood, childhood, adolescence, adulthood, old age

And the principles of fixed order and a first and last word also apply to the four seasons:

(8) spring, summer, autumn, winter

But the examples at (7) and (8) in fact represent two basic types of arrangement. In the first, we have pure linear ordering: B is next in sequence to A, C to B, and so on. Such sequences have been called **chain** sequences. In the second case, represented by the seasons, the sequences have all the characteristics just referred to, with a first word, a last word, and a fixed order. The differentiating feature is that if we take the sequence *spring, summer, autumn, winter, spring,* the first and last seasons mentioned do not take place in the same year (one spring might be in 2008, the other in 2009). In the course of one circuit (called a **spiral**) we have completed one year but also moved forward into the next.

Sometimes the rule prescribing a fixed first and last item is relaxed, and we have a **cycle**. In a cycle there are no outermost members: every member of the set is arranged between two others, as in the simplest type of 'colour circle' made up of segments of *red, purple, blue, green, yellow,* and *orange.* Here there is no starting-point and no end point. You will notice, though, that the circle is made up of three primary colours (*red, blue,* and *yellow*) and three secondary colours (*purple, green,* and *orange*) and that, in one form of the circle at least, each secondary colour is placed between the primaries of which it is composed (so *purple* between *red* and *blue*). You will recognize though, that unlike the colour circle, which is specially constructed, the rainbow is a natural phenomenon in which the colours appear in a band, with a first and last member (red and violet). It thus forms a chain.

A further ordering principle, leading to another major category, states that while the sequences involved will have a first and a last word, like chains and spirals, those sequences will also represent 'degrees of a property along a scale'—some characteristic such as size, rank, maturity, or academic success. So in the case of physical maturity in humans, for instance, it will be possible to say: 'a child is more mature than an infant', 'an adolescent is more mature than a child', and 'an adult is more mature than an adolescent'. Rank belongs in this major category, too, and we can remind ourselves that any one rank, say in the army, can be defined by reference to its neighbours on either side:

(9) A sergeant is senior to a corporal but junior to a colour-sergeant.

Closely similar to ranks are the names given to students in each of the four years of an American degree programme: *freshman, sophomore*, *junior*, and *senior*. As with military ranks, each name represents a discrete jump forward, while someone's status can be defined with reference to the level just above and/or below. Unlike ranks, however, a particular name corresponds to the student's year of study: sophomores are second-year students, and no particular merit attaches to their promotion!

5
Set phrases

The chief focus of previous chapters has been the meaning of single words, whether simple (like *book*) or complex (like *bookish* or *bookseller*). But lexical meaning is not only expressed by single words. It is also conveyed by well-established combinations of words—by **set phrases**. All phrases are of course made up of two or more words, but those we are now concerned with are not the kind that are put together to fit the needs of the moment, for example, *our striped wallpaper*, *his purple shirt*, or *her weekend job*, but the sort that are repeated and, through constant repetition, stored in our memories as more or less frozen units, for instance, *a shrinking violet*, *pass the buck*, *gain entry*, *a narrow escape*. So we are entering not so much the field of lexical creativity as the domain of the ready-made.

It means that we are faced with a difficulty. If our concern is chiefly with phrases that are memorized as wholes, how can they be said to relate to semantics? The answer can be found in two crucial points of contact between semantics and the study of phrases (**phraseology**). The first is that while set phrases form a separate part of the lexicon (and in fact have specialized dictionaries devoted to them) there are, between words on the one hand, and phrases on the other, many individual connections of the kind we described in the previous chapter as 'meaningful relations'. So, for example, *in focus* has as its synonyms *sharp* and *clear*, while *in the open* has as its one-word equivalents *revealed* or *disclosed*. And just as *fashionable* is the synonym of *in fashion*, so *unfashionable* (the opposite of *fashionable*, of course) is the synonym of *out of fashion*. Such meaningful linkages between words and set phrases are commonplace.

A second point of contact between phraseology and lexical semantics concerns the way that phrases with literal meanings develop into idioms. As we saw in Chapter 3, a device commonly used in developing new word-meanings is metaphor. The meanings of a great many phrases evolve in the same way, except that here the whole expression is involved. Take the phrase *play one's cards right*: to a card-player, this means 'to play one's cards appropriately, to the best advantage'. But by a metaphorical shift it has come to mean 'make the best use of one's assets and opportunities' generally. The literal phrase has become an idiom. When the verb *play*, incidentally, or the noun *card*, has to do with card games, there is an array of phrases with developed figurative senses: *play one's trump card*, for instance, *play one's cards close to one's chest*, and *not be playing with a full deck* (a US equivalent of *not having all one's marbles*).

Set phrases and set sentences

To carry the discussion a stage further, it will be helpful to set up a simple framework to account for the various types of set expression found in the language. Despite differences over terminology, specialists broadly agree in recognizing a basic division between 'set phrases' which have just been briefly introduced, and which are divided into **collocations** and idioms, and **set sentences**, which can be divided into a number of traditional categories, typically of sentence length, including proverbs (*make the punishment fit the crime*), catchphrases (*round up the usual suspects*), and slogans (*Heineken refreshes the parts other beers cannot reach*).

Set phrases and set sentences differ not only because the latter are potentially longer and more complex—look again at the examples just given and compare *turn up the heat* (idiom) and *if you can't stand the heat, get out of the kitchen* (catchphrase)—but because they have different uses and convey different kinds of meanings. Set phrases are word-combinations, more or less fixed in form, that function as parts of simple sentences, as can be seen from: *a sacred cow*, a noun phrase that can function as a subject or object; *on the loose*, a prepositional phrase that can be an adverbial; and *rush one's fences*, which fits a verb + object-noun pattern. Set sentences, by contrast, have meanings that largely reflect the way they function, as wholes, in spoken or written communication. The advertising slogan *all we do is driven by you*, for instance, combines two claims—that we make the car you drive, and that we are always motivated by our customers' wishes—in a succinct and witty form. But the range of sentence categories we regularly use goes some way beyond the traditional set. There are, for instance, expressions used to convey a speaker's reactions to other people and their messages, which include *Are you with me?*, *You know what I mean*, and *You must be joking!* These are called **speech formulae**, or 'gambits', and part of this extensive range will be dealt with in more detail later in the chapter.

Collocations

Collocations are by far the largest group of set phrases in English and, although awareness of them has not until fairly recently become widespread, they now serve as a constant reminder that much of the language we use from day to day is ready-made, as distinct from freshly minted by the application of semantic rules. Familiar examples of collocations are *gain entry*, *concede defeat*, *suffer a shock*, or, to change the pattern, *a blind alley*, *a golden opportunity*, *a narrow escape*.

Those examples illustrate the two most significant facts about this type of set phrase. A collocation is memorized as a lexical unity, but at the same time it is typically divided in two, both semantically and grammatically. The semantic division is clear from the fact that the nouns in both sets of examples are used in a literal sense: *entry* means 'entrance', *alley* 'a type of street', and so on. By contrast, the verbs in the first set and the adjectives in the second have a meaning that is often metaphorical. The nouns, with their literal meanings, can of course occur independently. In the collocations, though, they have a special function. Notice how the noun of *a narrow escape*, for instance, 'shapes' the meaning of the adjective to something like 'as if with little room to spare'.

In addition, collocations are typically pairs of words fitting a grammatical pattern. As we have seen, these are verb + noun and adjective + noun, though other types, such as verb + adverb (for example, *fail miserably*), are also found. An approach to collocations which takes account of the ways they function grammatically is valuable for two reasons. First, it makes us aware that while an adjective + noun collocation (say) may appear in a plural form (so, *blind alleys, golden opportunities, narrow escapes*) it is less likely to occur in a reversal of the basic pattern (i.e. noun + adjective): **the alley was blind, *the opportunity was golden, *the escape was narrow*. This is a good indication that we are dealing with collocations, because being memorized as words in a particular order, collocations often resist such switching about. In this respect they are unlike ordinary 'free combinations', as the following examples show: *a ripe apple, ripe apples, the apple was ripe; a bright pupil, bright pupils, the pupil was bright*.

There is a further advantage to be had from taking account of the grammatical patterning of collocations. For each combination of the verb + noun type (say), the grammar presents us with two major 'slots', in which, for any example, we can attempt to substitute verbs and/or nouns. The extent to which this is possible tells us how 'free' or how 'collocational' the example is.

We can see how this works in practice with the combination *open the door*. Here, the choice of nouns in the second slot (*door, gate, hatch*, etc.) is exceptionally wide. As a result the choices open to a speaker can be accounted for by means of a very general definition ('a hinged, sliding, or revolving barrier at the entrance to a building'). Here, then, we have a 'free combination', not a collocation.

With collocations, the range of choice tends to be more tightly constrained. Though many collocations can be easily understood, because of the literal meaning of one word in each case, a characteristic feature is limited choice at one or both points. Take the pairs *light rain, heavy rain*, and *light exercise, *heavy exercise*. The existence of both *light* and *heavy* in collocation with *rain* is to be expected, given the climatic extremes the British regularly experience, but while a strenuous workout in the gym certainly seems to qualify for the description *heavy exercise*, the actual collocation is seldom used. (Indeed, it fails to show up in the British National Corpus.) The explanation for this oddness seems to lie in the circumstances in which collocations are typically formed.

Once a collocation such as *light exercise* catches on (its seven BNC appearances are all in a 'healthier living' context), repetitive use may well follow, helping to fix the chosen form in the minds of speakers. But constant use also seems to have the effect in many cases of isolating the phrase from potential semantic neighbours, in this case *heavy exercise*, which might otherwise come into existence.

It might seem from examples like *open the door*, on the one hand, and (say) *deliver a lecture*, on the other, that the difference between free combinations and collocations is clear-cut. The reality is that the difference is in the nature of a gradation, or continuum. It is true, for example, that the range of object nouns used after the verb *deliver*, used in the figurative meaning 'present to an audience', is largely limited to *address*, *speech*, *lecture* (*talk* or *lesson* being improbable, because informal). However, the range of choice after the equally figurative *abandon* ('no longer support or believe') is wider and certainly not confined to *principle*, *idea*, *belief*, *doctrine*, *rule*, *claim*, *assertion*. Though the individual phrases that can be formed from both these lists are collocations because of the meanings of the verbs, those made up from the second list come closer to being free combinations.

Once the pairing of *abandon* and *belief*, say, has been lodged in a person's memory it makes for fluency of expression, since the speaker now has a ready-made, conventional way of conveying a particular verb-meaning in a given noun-context. We need to emphasize *conventional* way. The ability to produce the right pairing of words, like *mount an exhibition*, is a form of socially approved behaviour, and rather like 'good' manners, becomes self-effacing once acquired.

Idioms

The examples we saw a moment ago remind us of a defining difference between collocations and **idioms**. While collocations have a figurative meaning that takes in only *part* of the phrase, as in *deliver* (figurative) *a speech* (literal), in an idiom (see again *play one's cards right*) the figurative shift extends over the entire phrase.

What are the other key characteristics of idioms? Idioms originate in phrases with a literal meaning which have settled firmly into the lexicon through repeated use. Many 'literal phrases' remain in constant circulation over considerable periods, unchanged in form and meaning (*spread the butter, carve the joint, peel the potatoes*). It is arguable that many of these, rather than being made up afresh on each occasion of use, are simply stored and recalled as wholes.

Some of these phrases pass on into the next stage of development. They are figuratively extended, in terms of the whole expression, as has just been pointed out, but may or may not also preserve their original literal sense. Phrases that originated in the development of the railway network, such as *go/run off the rails*, reach the end of the line, and *run into/hit the buffers*, and which are now idiomatic, are among those which will still be understood in both a literal and a figurative sense by many speakers. These are the so-called 'figurative idioms'.

At the end of this particular line are those idioms whose figurative meanings, through constant use over the years, have congealed or ossified. Their senses can no longer be traced from the original literal ones (consider *pull one's socks up, an eager beaver, an ivory tower*).

Looking again along the line of development, we see a continuum extending from much repeated and memorized literal phrases, to items whose senses are partially intelligible, often because a once-fresh metaphor is not yet dead ('figurative idioms'), to those phrases whose meanings are impenetrable or opaque ('pure idioms'). According to those criteria, *mend one's fences* and *be meat and drink to somebody* are 'figurative', while *rush one's fences* and *grease someone's palm* are 'pure'.

We saw earlier how one of the means of distinguishing collocations from free combinations was to ask how flexible their grammar was. Since we were unable to say *the alley was blind* (as a 'transformation' of *a blind alley*) the example was to that extent a collocation. Does the same approach help us to distinguish one kind of idiom from another? The difficulty with this approach lies in finding the right restrictions to do the diagnostic work. Consider the active to passive switch in pure idioms such as *spill the beans* and *grease someone's palm*. It happens that both can be passivized—compare *the beans were spilt, his palm was greased*. But the opposite is true of *fit the bill* or *kick the bucket*. We must simply accept that near the upper end of the continuum, the results of various tests may pull in different directions. This is as true of meaning and substitution within the idiom as of anything else. So the following phrases are opaque semantically, while allowing a small number of fixed substitutes: *Shanks's pony/mare*, *the rough edge/side of one's tongue*, *a chink/crack in one's armour*.

Proverbs, catchwords, and formulae

Let us now go back to the major grouping referred to earlier as 'set sentences'. Proverbs form an interesting category, as many have undergone structural changes over the past half-century, while many have virtually disappeared from our vocabularies. Anyone searching the British National Corpus for the proverbs *man proposes, but God disposes* or *one man's meat is another man's poison*, for example, will be disappointed. There is no record of either occurring even once in a body of 100 million words. Interestingly, even among those proverbs that do survive, there are many with living heads but chopped-off tails, such as *too many cooks*, *a stitch in time*, *bolt the stable door*. From full sentences they have been reduced to phrases or clauses. Now, it is true that when these truncated forms are used, the unspoken ending is in most cases also implied, as here: *too many cooks spoil the broth* and *a stitch in time saves nine*. The part that survives conveys the meaning of the whole. Nevertheless, it seems that complete proverbs are less and less often used, perhaps as a reflection of our unwillingness to take seriously such encapsulations of folk wisdom, or to recognize them as guides to personal conduct.

Catchphrases claim our interest because of the way they come into existence and, in many cases, subsequently take on fresh uses and forms. They commonly originate with a popular entertainer or public figure (when they fulfil much the same function as a signature tune) or a character in a well-known film or television drama series. In the film *Casablanca*, 'Round up the usual suspects!' was an order given to police officers to arrest a number of people they had often arrested before, not because anyone believed they had committed any crime, but because the police wished to appear active and efficient. For many filmgoers it thereafter became inseparable from the cynical and corrupt police chief (Captain Renault) by whom the words were first spoken and the catchphrase was coined. The meaning of the original expression has broadened, so that it can now refer to the persistent targeting of a wide variety of people or things (as in the following quotation), and not simply helpless refugees:

(1) Excise duties are taxes on specific goods, with cigarettes, booze, and petrol being *the usual suspects* to be *rounded up* on Budget Day.

I suggested earlier that the spread of sentence-length items extended well beyond the traditional categories of proverbs, catchphrases, and slogans. Among this wider and less familiar range of set sentences is one without which spoken and written communication would be less smooth and coherent. The term **speech formula** or 'gambit' is used to refer to these invaluable items. Speech formulae are expressions, typically spanning a whole sentence or clause, that are used to convey a speaker's assessment of other participants and their messages, and generally to ease the flow of discourse. Examples include *I beg your pardon, Are you with me?, You know what I mean?*, and *call it what you like*.

What are the distinguishing features of these speech formulae? All four examples can occur as separate sentences (*I beg your pardon?, You know what I mean?*, and so on) and all are used to perform some kind of 'act' with language. Saying *I beg your pardon*, for example, may (it has more than one meaning) be a response to something just said by another speaker; specifically, it can function as a request for clarification, as here:

(2) 'We're in trouble if it won't fit in.' '*I beg your pardon*, if it won't fit in what?'

Whether the speech formulae appear on their own or not, they typically form part of a verbal *interaction*. And incidentally, it is not always the case that the formula is a response to something that someone else has said or asked. They are more than likely to be interactive in some other way. Look at this example:

(3) 'Now, these firms, they'd got <u>a certain type of lock</u> that they produced, and it was all done with <u>a system</u>, *you know what I mean?*

Here, the formula, which is in end position, is addressed to a listener, but it aims to check that he or she has understood the meanings of *a certain type of lock* and *a system*, which are not spelt out. So the formula relates both to the hearer and to parts of the language of the speaker. In a final example, the formula *if you please* is not used to seek for confirmation that the speaker has been understood, but rather is signalling his or her judgement that the preceding claim is absurd or unreasonable and no doubt also that the audience is expected to agree:

(4) The parents want some say in the fate of their children and these days even the children demand to be heard, *if you please*.

Set phrases and creativity

Clustering at the upper end of the **scale of idiomaticity** is a group of phrases that are invariable in structure and opaque in meaning. However, some of their near neighbours may also be opaque, and yet allow a few substitutes, as in *save one's own neck/skin*. Partly because they are so few, the substitutes are seen as well-established, memorized parts of the idioms, so that a creative reshaping of one of them can produce the same shock effect as when an invariable phrase is involved.

Quality newspapers are an expected source of such 'nonce' (coined for the occasion) variation. Educated readers, it can be assumed, are linguistically sharp enough to recognize that in the headline *Pharaoh's museum hopes to shelter reigning cats and dogs* (a reference to plans to dedicate a room in a Cairo museum to mummified royal pets), the well-known idiom is not on the surface but underlies an appropriate recasting of forms and meanings.

Despite the undoubted appeal of such verbal play, however, nonce manipulation of idioms, proverbs, and catchphrases is somewhat rare, though more common in some genres, such as the city pages and sports columns, than others (and altogether more frequent in the tabloid press as a whole). What is much more characteristic of quality newspaper texts is the widespread and unmodified use of collocations.

Of all types of set phrases, it is collocations that make the most significant contribution to educated written proficiency in English. They are, for instance, pervasive in the language of the social sciences, as a number of studies have shown. Some analyses of such texts have put the percentage of collocations as high as 35 per cent of all combinations of a given structural pattern. What explains this preference? One useful property of non-creative collocations is that they represent a neutral ('unmarked') option and help to produce an unobtrusive style that suggests objectivity. They therefore commend themselves to people in public life, including serious commentators and academics, who wish to convey such characteristics in their writing. Collocations play an important role in setting a particular neutral stamp on educated written prose.

The value of the 'marked' option, by contrast (the creatively modified idiom, formula, or catchphrase), is that it draws attention away from the content of a text and on to its form, and in newspaper editorials, for example, provides scope for witty comment and evaluation.

6
Components of meaning

Chapter 4, on 'meaningful relations', demonstrated one approach to explaining the meanings of words in an orderly and informative way. The discussion focused on words as wholes and showed how they were systematically related to one another. *Married* and *single*, for example, were shown to be opposites (specifically 'complementaries'), while *potato* and *cassava* were shown to be 'co-hyponyms' of *tuber*. A different approach altogether would be to move 'inside' words, as it were, and break down their meanings into fragments or components, such as 'male' and 'female' or 'adult' and 'non-adult'. This is the approach to the study of meaning known as **componential analysis**. We are drawing on it when we say that the meaning of *mare* is made up of the components 'female' and 'horse' and that of *foal* of the components 'non-adult' and 'horse'. The particular strength of a componential approach is that while it is effective in analysing groups of words (such as the names of members of a family) that are systematic, it is also helpful in throwing light on groupings of words (such as the names of pieces of household furniture) that defy neat analysis.

Componential analysis

If we start from the idea that the meanings of words can be broken down into a number of abstract components or **semantic features,** our task is to identify those features that will distinguish the meaning of any one word from every other that might (as one linguist has put it) 'compete for a place in the same semantic territory'. For example, *boy* and *girl* belong together because they share the features 'human' and 'non-adult' and differ only in that *girl* combines 'female' with those two features, rather than 'male'. In a similar way, *armchair* and *sofa* have in common the features 'with a back' and 'with arms', and so share territory with each other, too. They differ chiefly in the fact that *armchair* has the component 'for one person' rather than 'for more than one'.

This general approach to describing semantically-related words has a long history in Europe. In America, though, componential analysis was first adopted not by linguists, but by anthropologists, as a method of analysing and comparing kinship terms. As a relatively simple case, consider *maternal aunt* and *paternal uncle*, where we need to take account of the gender of the person referred to and her (or his) sibling relationship with the mother (or father) of the speaker (the 'ego'). But it has proved fruitful to apply componential analysis to a number of other domains, too, including the names of animal species distinguished by sex, adulthood, and parentage. So, if we focus on the variable 'adulthood', we have:

(1) *Cat* is to *kitten*, as *dog* is to *pup/puppy*, as *horse* is to *foal* (i.e. as 'adult' is to 'non-adult').

This particular series can of course be extended to include (say) *pig* and *piglet*, where *piglet* has the separable suffix *-let*, and so is a case of word-formation (see Chapter 2), though nevertheless analysable as 'non-adult'. And notice too the derivative *puppy*, which for some speakers is more informal and affectionate than *pup*.

Of course, if we make a different choice of variable, here 'sex', another series can be captured:

(2) *Boar* is to *sow*, as *stallion* is to *mare*, as *bull* is to *cow* (i.e. as 'male' is to 'female').

Finally, the semantic contrasts that together define a particular word meaning can be gathered together to form a 'componential definition', like this:

(3) *boy*: + 'human' – 'adult' + 'male'; *girl*: + 'human' – 'adult' – 'male'.

Why the pluses and minuses? If you look back at the examples at (2), you will see that the contrast between 'male' and 'female' is expressed by using precisely those two words as semantic labels. But in some cases it is appropriate, as well as more economical, to express a contrast in terms of plus or minus values (say, +/–'adult') of the same variable ('adulthood'). But what about 'female' represented as –'male'? There are two possible objections here. Fair-minded readers of both sexes may very well object to seeing femaleness apparently defined as the absence of maleness. And some at least of the objectors might be satisfied by seeing 'male' represented as –'female'! But this misses the point. The contrast between *boy* and *girl*, say, is not a relationship between two words one of which indicates some positive property and the other its absence. The pair *dead* and *alive*, or *enslaved* and *free*, illustrate *that* kind of contrast (and the *dead* to *alive* opposition is correctly represented as –/+ 'alive'). The contrast between the words *boy* and *girl*, though, is a relationship in which each of the opposites denotes a *positive* property. And the appropriate way to express that contrast is to use 'male' and 'female'.

Marked and unmarked

We are faced with an additional and different kind of semantic contrast when describing *dog* in relation to *bitch*. For, on the one hand, it is possible to say *this isn't a bitch, it's a dog* (which clearly identifies the animal in question as 'male'), while on the other we can say *there were ten dogs in the room but only one was a bitch*, which makes equally clear that the bitch that happens to be present can also be referred to as a dog. How do we account for this lopsidedness in the meanings of the words? One part of the answer is to recognize that the 'male' versus 'female' distinction that we talked about earlier can apply in this case also. It, too, is a straightforward example of componential contrast, reflected in the example *this isn't a bitch, it's a dog* (and also in *this isn't a vixen, it's a fox*).

But what of the other half of the picture? *Vixen* and *bitch* refer only to females (in componential terms they are always 'female'), and are thus **marked**. On the other hand, *fox* and *dog* can refer, in various contexts, to males *or* females, and are thus **unmarked**. The phrases *male dog* and *female dog* are both acceptable. In those contexts the contrast in terms of 'male' and 'female' between *dog* and *bitch* has clearly broken down.

In English it is common to find that the word referring to the female is marked, as in *tiger/tigress*; *lion/lioness*; *deer/doe* (and, in French, *tigre/tigresse*; *lion/lionne*; *cerf/biche*). Notice, incidentally, that the 'femaleness' of *lioness* and *lionne* is conveyed by the visible suffixes *-ess* and *-ne*, while that of *doe* and *biche* is captured by invisible features. This is one case among several, in both languages, where the same contrast is expressed by different means. It is worth pointing out also that it is not always the word referring to the female that is marked. For example, among domesticated animals and birds, in France as well as in Britain, it is often the case that the word that denotes the male is marked. So in English, *bull* is marked in relation to *cow* and *cock* (or *cockerel*) in relation to *hen*. (Compare *taureau/vache* and *coq/poule*.) The explanation seems to be that the males of these species are kept on farms in smaller numbers, and then chiefly for breeding. The main animal and bird populations are female and their names treated as unmarked within the lexicons of both English and French. (See Chapter 4.)

Some advantages of a componential approach

It is not only fields involving two or three variables, such as those we have just been looking at, that can be dealt with by means of componential analysis. On the contrary, this approach enables us to open up complex areas of the lexicon, including some that do not lend themselves readily to analysis in terms of hyponymy ('branching hierarchies') but which do bring to light several types of semantic contrast, including stylistic and emotive variables. Exploring descriptive problems to which componential analysis seems to offer informative solutions will take up the remainder of this chapter.

We might ask at the outset how far the members of a particular field (say, 'items of household furniture') can be fitted into a tree diagram, as used in Chapter 4 to demonstrate the hyponymous links between the names of vegetables. The group of items we shall look at includes, as a basic list, *seat*, *chair*, *armchair*, *stool*, *sofa*, and *bench*, though, as we shall see, *carver* is also a candidate for inclusion. In terms of the 'meaningful relations' explored in Chapter 4, *seat* is clearly identifiable as the

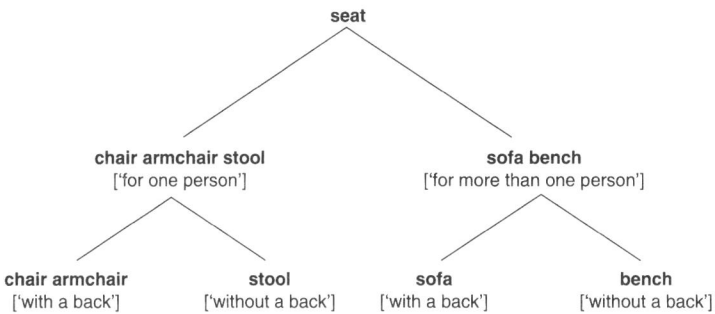

FIGURE 6.1 *Tentative tree diagram for the 'seat' domain*

superordinate term (*this is an armchair* implies *this is a seat*, but *this is a seat* does not imply *this is an armchair*), and it is *seat* that heads the following tentative tree diagram.

As can be seen, the various items are set out in bold print while semantic features in terms of which they can be contrasted appear in square brackets. As a first level below *seat*, we might recognize a distinction between seats for one person (for example, *chair*, *armchair*, *stool*) and seats for more than one (*sofa*, *bench*). Intuitively, that seems the right way to start.

But below that level the difficulties begin, since if we now wish to make a further division on the basis of 'with a back' and 'without a back', say, we find we have to make it on *both* sides of the existing split. This must be done to take account of the fact that while stools and benches differ in the amount of seating they provide, they are alike in *lacking* support for the back. Armchairs and sofas, though, while also differing in the amount of seating each provides, are alike in *giving* support to the back. At this point, we can see that tree diagrams of the kind we have already met are not well suited to capturing the kinds of contrasts which surface in some semantic fields.

Because of these complexities, a framework other than the tree-diagram has to be used. It is best to arrange the features in a **matrix**, which is a grid with the lexical items arranged down one side and the semantic components set out across the top (see Table 6.1). This makes no claim to being a symmetrical arrangement, as a tree diagram might, but it does incorporate all the relevant distinctions for the six items in a way that makes them easy to examine and compare. With one exception, 'for one person/for two or more persons', '+' represents in the matrix the presence of the property in question (a back and arms in the case of an armchair, legs in the case of a stool) and '–' its absence. The zero ('o') indicates that the relevant choice cannot be made because the conditions for it do not exist (the presence of a back and arms if padding is to be specified).

One further point. There may be differences in what individual speakers choose to call a particular item of furniture, or indeed whether they believe that a separate name should be assigned to it at all. What for example do we call a chair that has arms but no padding at the back and sides? (The kind of chair in which I am comfortably seated at the moment.) Is this nonetheless an armchair? For me, it is. However, if a similar chair with arms is the principal chair in a dining-room, the one intended for the person carving meat, it is recognized by many people as a *carver*, and is so designated in standard dictionaries. Such uncertainty or vagueness is not unusual. It is found in many parts of the lexicon, especially where, as here, a new use for an object is pulling in one direction, and what is felt to be its characteristic shape is pulling in another.

To show how the complexity of a **lexical field** and the nature of its components can vary from one domain to another, one

	one person/ two or more (1/2+)	with/ without a back	with/ without legs	with/ without arms	with/ without padding on back and arms
seat	1/2+	+/–	+/–	+/–	+/–
chair	1	+	+	–	+/–
armchair	1	+	+/–	+	+
stool	1	–	+	–	o
sofa	2+	+	+/–	+	+
bench	2+	–	+	–	o

TABLE 6.1 *Matrix for the* seat *domain*

of the most useful groupings is of words denoting 'movement across the ground'. To begin with, we need to limit the range of movements to those of human beings, to avoid having to deal with such additional variables as the hopping of frogs and the dancing of trained bears. Those meanings would be analysed separately. Then, despite a common tendency to contrast *run* and *walk* in terms of speed, the key distinguishing feature for these and other verbs is the nature of the contact between the feet and the ground. With *run*, *hop*, *skip*, and *jump*, and some uses of *dance* (especially among ballet dancers), there are times when neither foot is in contact with the ground. With *walk* and other uses of *dance* (especially among ballroom dancers), at least one foot is always in contact. The contrast between 'one foot or the other always in contact' and 'neither foot at times in contact' can be expressed by the use of 'plus' and 'minus'.

But even more specific is the order in which the feet make contact with the ground (an aspect of the overall meaning which the '+/–' distinction is incapable of representing). For *run* and *walk*, the order of contact is 1–2–1–2 (and so on); for *hop*, the order is 1–1–1 or 2–2–2; while for *skip*, the order is 1–1–2–2. And that is the form in which the types of alternation characteristic of the verbs are recorded in Table 6.2.

Verbs	1 One foot or the other always in contact, versus neither foot at times in contact	2 Order of contact	3 Number of limbs involved
run	–	1–2–1–2	2
walk	+	1–2–1 –2	2
hop	–	1–1–1 or 2–2–2	1
skip	–	1–1–2–2	2
jump	–	not relevant	2
dance	+/–	variable but rhythmic	2

TABLE 6.2 *Matrix for 'movement across the ground'*

Denotation and connotation

This survey of componential analysis has focused up to this point on 'denotative' meaning, or those aspects of meaning which have to do with literal, primary relationships between words or phrases, on the one hand, and objects, states, or events, on the other. **Denotation** is usually given priority of treatment in semantics because, as we have seen, it often has a complex organization that lends itself to systematic analysis. The relations of dependency (say, between *armchair* and *seat*) and contrast (say, between *sofa* and *bench*) that we have seen displayed in Table 6.1, and which involve denotative features, are evidence of such structuring.

Connotation, on the other hand, has to do with aspects of meaning which are less easy to treat componentially. Yet they are nevertheless established properties of words and phrases, and knowledge of them is essential for successful communication. Denotation constitutes the basic conceptual level of meaning, connotation the equally vital associative level. As an aspect of the latter, take the important category of 'evaluation'. The choice of an evaluative word or phrase implies a particular attitude (approving, disapproving, and so on) towards the person or thing referred to. The adjective *slender*, for instance, indicates approval or admiration of a thin person (usually a young woman) so described; *skinny* suggests the opposite. In this case, though, two relationships are involved. *Slender* and *skinny* are opposed to each other, connotatively, in terms of 'approving' versus 'disapproving'; and they are jointly related to *thin*, also connotatively, as the 'neutral' term (i.e. neither approving nor disapproving).

Another aspect of connotation is **level of formality**. Here we consider the close or distant personal relationships which call for particular forms of address. For example, one might address a woman police officer of a particular rank as *ma'am*, *inspector*, *Inspector Tennison*, *Jane*, or *guv'nor* depending on one's relative seniority (*Jane* suggests senior to junior, or 'of equivalent rank', and *ma'am* junior to senior). But other factors come into play. Formality can be dissolved by the camaraderie of an investigative team, so *ma'am* can give way to *guv'nor*, or *guv* (and *sergeant* to *skipper*, or *skip*).

Connotation is well suited to the analysis of lexical fields since connotative features often serve to distinguish members of a field that are identical in denotation (*marry*, *wed*, *get hitched*, for instance, all refer to the same kind of event). Notice that connotative features are essentially **gradable** (that is, describable in terms of 'more' or 'less') in relation to semantic groupings of words. Consider *live together*, *cohabit*, *shack up*, *live in sin*, for example, whose relative formality has been represented, in one study, as points along a numbered scale, with 'o' as the mid-point. So, *live together* can be described as 'neutral' (o), *cohabit* as 'fairly formal' (+1), *shack up* as 'very informal' (−3), and *live in sin* as 'fairly informal' (−1). It is worth noting, though, that *live in sin* must be on more than one scale, since for many people it is humorous as well as old-fashioned (the former, perhaps, because of the latter). And compare *cohabit*, which is 'fairly formal' but also possibly 'legal'.

The difference between two sets of meanings, one of which has no special overtones while the other is disparaging, or disapproving (and hence connotative) may come about through the development of metaphors. Take the 'trap the unwary' meanings of *snare*, *hook*, and *trap*, which have developed as metaphors from individual literal meanings concerned with trapping or catching game or fish. To speak of 'snaring' or 'hooking' a husband or wife is only made sense of by applying a 'transfer rule' whereby the metaphorical meaning of *snare* (or *hook*) is interpreted as 'act in a way that is similar to catching an animal or fish'. The 'ground' of the similarity (see also Chapter 3) can be formulated, in componential terms, as features common to the literal and figurative senses, for example: + 'subject gains', + 'prey typically unaware', + 'with skill and/or cunning'.

However, this metaphorical shift has also brought about an association between the new figurative meaning and evaluation. In the case of *snare*, *hook*, and *trap*, the subject (or 'doer') will be assumed to have acted in an underhand or calculating way. In a componential treatment, the verb meanings would be rated + 'disapproving' or + 'scornful'.

At the beginning of this chapter, I suggested that a particular strength of the componential approach was its flexibility. It could be effective in describing, in a systematic way, words that were intuitively related, such as the names of wild or domestic animals and birds. But it could also throw light on groupings of words, denoting, say, 'movement across the ground', by recognizing different kinds of variable, and making use of special kinds of label, or combinations of labels. In dealing with both those cases, we were at the same time concentrating on the literal, denotative level of meaning (on sofas and armchairs, say, as seats with arms and padding) and not on the associative, connotative level (sitting-room furniture as a focus of domestic comfort and warmth). But as those examples may show, connotations are also established properties of words, and fully part of our semantic knowledge as native speakers.

7
Semantics and the dictionary

From time to time in this book, while progressing from one descriptive approach to another, we have turned to a dictionary entry to illustrate a semantic point. This should come as no surprise. The most commonly owned work of reference in the average home or office is a dictionary—a medium-sized, mother-tongue 'desk' dictionary—and this, despite the attractions of online resources, is in no danger of being supplanted as an organized, accessible source of information about the lexicon.

But the desk dictionary has qualities beyond ready availability and handy size to commend it. One interesting feature is that several of the definition types, and the rigorous style of defining, that we have found in the work of linguists are to be found much earlier in conventional dictionaries. We saw, for example, in Chapter 4 that to explain a meaning we often use a short phrase containing a more general word than the one we wish to explain. As an instance, we took the phrase 'a hornbeam is a tree...', pointing out that this was an approach widely adopted in dictionaries. In fact, the example formed the opening of a specific dictionary definition.

This chapter will summarize the major themes of the book. But there is much to be said for reviewing them against the background of a desk dictionary. Various parallels and cross-currents come to mind. One point is that dictionaries are typically organized to throw light on meanings, so a major imperative is to ensure that readers have quick access to that information. But as we shall see, this orientation will sometimes cut across meaningful connections that a linguist might wish to emphasize.

Grammatical and lexical items

Though 'grammatical items' were introduced in the opening chapter of this book, the chief emphasis throughout has been on lexical items and the complex words they can be used to form, the meaningful relations they enter into, and so on. Grammatical items have not been lost sight of. It is simply that in a book of modest size it is difficult to do full justice to grammatical items when lexical items are so much more numerous and complex. Let us, though, turn our attention briefly to **grammatical items**, partly to remind ourselves of their characteristic features, and partly to show how they interact with lexical items.

Grammatical items fall into a number of classes, of which articles (*the*, *a/an*), possessives (*his*, *her*), prepositions (*above*, *between*), and modal verbs (*might*, *should*), are among the most familiar. These groupings have a number of features in common. Though the overall number of grammatical items is small compared with the number of lexical items, their frequency of occurrence is much higher, a fact that a glance at corpus data will quickly confirm. Second, their membership tends to be stable, while that of lexical items tends to expand in response to changes in the objects and events they refer to. Both these characteristics reflect a common purpose: the use of grammatical items as a kind of cement, holding sentences and phrases together and so providing a structural framework within which lexical items can express a constantly varying semantic content. We can see from the following skeleton of a noun phrase, for instance, how the first *the* and the prepositional phrase *of the ... ahead* form the outer framework for the 'head' noun *stage*, and how the second *the* begins to form a second frame for *campaign*:

Determiner + Numeral + Head noun + Prepositional phrase
The   *second*   stage   *of the* campaign *ahead*

Complex words

In dealing earlier with complex words (word-formation), we saw that there were three kinds of processes at work. First, there was the development by which simple words such as *rain* and *work* had small elements called prefixes and suffixes added to them to form complex words, or derivatives (in this case, *rainy*, *worker*). Then there was the process known as conversion, by which a lexical item (say, *plaster*, noun) was made a member of another word-class without adding a prefix or suffix (compare *plaster*, verb). Both kinds of process could be contrasted with compounding, which involved the addition of one simple word to another (for example, *book* to *shelf* to form *bookshelf*).

For the dictionary-maker there are various factors to be taken into account when deciding where and how complex items produced by derivation (including conversion) and compounding are to be treated in the structure of the dictionary. There are first questions of accessibility. A number of studies of dictionary use have shown that, whether they are native speakers or foreign learners, most users turn to the dictionary to find out the meaning (less often, the spelling) of a word or phrase. That being so, it seems sensible to list the derivatives of a simple word in alphabetical order *outside* the **main entry** for the word itself which, in the following sequence, is *defect*:

> **defect** *(n)* …
> **defection** … *(n)* …
> **defective** … *(adj)* …

Based on American principles, this has, since the late 1980s, become common practice among British makers of desk dictionaries. However, pressure on space often compels the lexicographer to modify this policy in some cases. Consider the suffixes *-ly* and *-ness*, whose **productivity** was mentioned in Chapter 2. Since these endings are freely employed in speech and writing to produce derivatives whose meanings are easily arrived at (compare *calm*, *calmly*, *calmness*), they are treated as **run-ons** in many dictionaries, that is, included within the entry for the simple word:

> **calm** … *(adj)* … – **calmly** *(adv)* – **calmness** *(n)*

In the dictionary treatment of *compounds* several competing pressures are at work. For ease of access, compounds will normally be treated alphabetically as main entries. And note, too, that when arranging the items, a derivative will interrupt a sequence of compounds if its spelling calls for it. In the following run, *motorable* is a derivative, and so too is *motorcade*, produced by **clipping** *cavalcade* and **blending** the clipped portion *-cade* with the simple word *motor*. And notice, finally, that there is no generally accepted rule governing the spelling of specific compounds. In the dictionary from which these examples were taken, *motorcar* is spelt as you see it, with the two elements joined (**solid**). But in another leading dictionary the preferred spelling is **open**, thus *motor car*.

> **motor** ... (*n*) ...
> **motorable** ... (*adj*) (of a road) suitable for use by motor vehicles.
> **motorbicycle** ... (*n*) ...
> **motorbike** ... (*n*) ...
> **motorbus** ... (*n*) ...
> **motorcade** ... (*n*) a parade of cars or other motor vehicles.
> **motor camp** ... (*n*) N.Z. a camp for motorists, tents, and caravans.
> **motorcar** ... (*n*) ...

Multiple meaning

One of the problems we are normally unaware of as ordinary speakers of English, but which interests lexicographers, is how to tell the difference between two words of identical form but completely separate meanings (or homonymy) and two words of the same form whose meanings are different but related (polysemy). As we saw in Chapter 3, various tests can help us separate off the more clear-cut cases, such as 'bank[1]' (the financial sense) and 'bank[2]' (the 'embankment' sense). (Here, a collocation such as 'draw cash/money from the X' will provide an acceptable context for one word but not the other.) But the important point to bear in mind is that most pairs we test in this way will not give clear-cut results. There is in fact a shading-off from homonymy, on the one hand, to meanings which though related are widely separated, on the other.

How are these differences and similarities conveyed in the dictionary? In Chapter 3, we saw how the internal organization of the dictionary entry 'mate[1]' (its **microstructure**) could reflect the way that meanings (including meanings due to metaphorical change) develop over time. In many dictionaries, numbers are used to indicate major sense-divisions, and letters minor shades of meaning. Comparison of the same set of meanings in two or more editions can of course show the stages at which new senses emerge. But sometimes the order of existing meanings is rearranged. It may be that editors have realized that a later meaning has largely supplanted an earlier one. This happened when the editor of the eighth edition of the *Concise Oxford Dictionary* (1990) became aware that the first sense of *aftermath* given in the previous edition of 1982 was no longer in general currency, and needed to be replaced as the principal meaning, as in the second excerpt here:

> **aftermath** ... (*n*) grass growing after mowing or harvest; (fig.) consequences (*the aftermath of war*). (1982)
> **aftermath** ... (*n*) 1 consequences; after-effects (*the aftermath of war*). 2 new grass growing after mowing or after a harvest. (1990)

The evidence on which this decision was based reflected the greater breadth and depth of the material assembled at Oxford University Press by the late 1980s, which included computer databases as well as printed material of all kinds. Continuing expansion since that time of text corpora (large bodies of written texts gathered on computers) has enabled dictionary-makers to claim with confidence that particular words and meanings have passed out of use altogether.

Meaningful relations

One descriptive approach, referred to as meaningful relations (technically, **sense relations**), is concerned with the semantic links which exist between pairs of words. One such pairing is 'converseness', illustrated by *husband/wife* and *teacher/pupil*. There are of course more complex groupings that words can belong to. The names of the seasons (*spring*, *summer*, *autumn*, and *winter*) form one particular grouping. Another, which typifies the way the names of vegetables, fruit, or flowers are semantically related, is made up of a general term, or 'superordinate' (say, *pulse*), and two or more specific terms, or 'hyponyms' (say, *lentil*, *chickpea*, and *bean*). Something close to this arrangement is familiar to dictionary users from a particular type of definition, one that works by providing examples of the thing being defined, as in the two entries below:

pulse[2] ... the edible seeds of various leguminous plants, for example, lentils, chickpeas, and beans.
tuber[1] ... the underground part of a plant, especially when fleshy and enlarged ... *e.g.* a turnip or carrot.

As it happens, there is no need to thank lexical semantics for these helpful arrangements. They come from within lexicography itself (the headwords with their definitions appeared in a pocket dictionary of 1946). It is a particular case of the two traditions coming together.

Componential analysis

For an example of lexical analysis which is the work of linguists and lexicographers and designed to help readers with their vocabulary development, consider the following 'matrix'. As we saw in Chapter 6 with verbs of motion (*skip*, *jump*, *hop*, etc.), a matrix consists of a set of lexical items which have a small number of semantic features in common, but which can then be distinguished by highly specific meanings. In the following matrix, taken from a dictionary, 'throw', 'in different directions', and 'deliberate' are the shared features (and *scatter* the most general item). But in other respects the items are related to and different from each other in highly specific ways: *scatter over* or *about* suggests that the action is careless and messy; *strew* (more commonly found in the form *strewn*) can be careless too, but the intention may be benign; *sprinkle* suggests small quantities scattered over a short range:

When we *scatter* something we throw it in different directions ... *Scatter over/about* suggests that the throwing is done carelessly and causes a mess: *Who's scattered my papers all over the floor?* ... *Strew* can suggest both intentional and careless throwing: *The streets were strewn with flowers for the royal visit. There was litter strewn all over the pavement. Sprinkle* is used with water, sand, salt, etc. and indicates intentional scattering, usually over a small area ...

Phraseology

Now consider the role played by collocations in that matrix. Each verb is accompanied by one or more collocates (like this: *sprinkle...water, sand, salt*), and they are of value in establishing the precise semantic contrasts between the verbs. But there is a further significant point. *Sprinkle water, sand*, and so on, fit the grammatical pattern verb + noun, and in that pattern substitutions can be made telling us more about specific collocations. Where the nouns that can accompany a verb such as *sprinkle* are relatively numerous (*salt, caster sugar, flour*, beside those already given), the collocations are relatively 'open' or 'free'. When, on the other hand, the possible choices are very few, we are dealing with collocations that are 'restricted'. (Compare: *govern feelings, passion, temper*, and see Chapter 5).

This is a view of collocation that was first developed by Russian linguists over 50 years ago, and that has subsequently influenced the design of collocational dictionaries in Russia and elsewhere, including Britain. However, especially in Britain since the early 1980s, a contrasting view has developed of what collocations are and how they should be identified in texts. This approach, which has been closely identified with the COBUILD project and its founder, John Sinclair, is that collocation is 'the co-occurrence of two or more words within a short distance of one another [i.e. with usually no more than four words intervening] in a text'.

If this definition is applied with absolute strictness, then *declined*, as the key term in the first example, forms collocations with the items *value, of, her*, and *currency*:

... the value of her currency declined
Britain's share of world shipbuilding had as a result declined
... population has in some cases actually declined
... the number of prairie fires actually declined

The first observation to make is that *of* and *her* are grammatical items that can combine with very many lexical items other than *currency*, say. They tell us very little about collocation. However, grammar has a more important part to play if we consider the roles of *value* and *currency* and their relative distance from *declined*. The noun *value* is farther from that key item (or **node**) than the noun *currency*, yet strictly it is the former, not the latter, which is the subject of the verb *declined*. In the same way (in the second example) it is the *share* of world shipbuilding that has declined and not shipbuilding as such. So the closeness, in terms of spaces, of a word to the node will not always help us if we are attempting to gather significant collocations.

Yet, there is no need to abandon a valuable asset—**corpus** data—when we are attempting to identify collocations and determine their relative frequency. However, we do need to insist on the added dimension of grammatical patterning. Many linguists involved in the study of phraseology now combine a dependence on corpus data with close attention to the grammatical patterns in which collocations are found. And sophisticated computer programs exist which can identify collocations in corpus texts in relation to their grammatical patterns.

Conclusions

Our chief aim in this book has been to introduce a number of distinctive, well-established approaches to the description of words and their meanings. Some attention has been given to grammatical items (and so to grammatical meanings) but throughout we have focused chiefly on the much larger number of lexical items that exist, and the correspondingly large spread of derivatives and compounds they give rise to. Each major approach, say, sense relations and componential analysis, has its own theoretical basis, but specific cases of overlap are found between one system and another, as when one of a pair of complementary terms, say *married* (of the pair *married/single*), is also a derivative of a simple verb (here, *marry*). These connections are captured in various standard dictionaries with entries that begin like this:

   unmarried (*adj*) not married; single ...

The particular aim of this final chapter has been to reconsider the major topics of the earlier sections against a background of tradition and innovation in dictionary-making. Well worth noting in this chapter were references to the use of corpus data when recording a new sense or to change the ordering of existing senses. But more encouraging still to the practising lexicographer is the present availability of a great range and diversity of online resources. With the insights that lexical semantics affords, and the ample evidence that the British National Corpus and other corpora provide, even the dictionary-maker working alone is well equipped to gather appropriate examples and make informed decisions as to which instances should form the basis of dictionary entries.

Readings

Chapter 1
Words and meanings

Text 1

RONALD CARTER: *Vocabulary: Applied Linguistic Perspectives*. Allen and Unwin 1987, page 8

The discussion in this passage focuses on the differences between lexical and grammatical items. There is a potentially infinite number of lexical words and, by contrast, a finite number of grammatical words. The two categories convey different kinds of meaning.

One distinction which it is clearly necessary to draw is that between grammatical and lexical words. The former comprise a small and finite class of words which includes pronouns (*I*, *you*, *me*), articles (*the*, *a*), auxiliary verbs (*must*, *could*, *shall*), prepositions (*in*, *on*, *with*, *by*) and conjunctions (*and*, *but*). *Grammatical words* like these are also variously known as 'functional words', 'functors', 'empty words'. *Lexical words*, on the other hand—which are also variously known as 'full words' or 'content words'—include nouns (*man*, *cat*), adjectives (*large*, *beautiful*), verbs (*find*, *wish*) and adverbs (*brightly*, *luckily*). They carry a higher information content and are syntactically structured by the grammatical words. Also, while there are a finite number of grammatical words, there is a potentially unlimited number of lexical words. It is lexical words, too, which are most subject to what linguists term diachronic change, that is, changes in form or meaning over a period of time. There are numerous examples of regular changes in meaning of lexical words in the course of the historical development of any language. But grammatical words remain generally more immutable. This gives some obvious ground, therefore, for linguists to be able to refer to lexical words as an *open class* of words while grammatical words constitute a *closed class*.

▷ *Why do you think lexical words are said to be 'full' and grammatical words 'empty'?*

▷ *Grammatical words are said to change very little, in form, meaning, or use over time. Comment on the use of the pronoun 'one' in 'One must sympathize with her', and of the possessive determiner 'their' in 'Someone has left their bike outside'.*

Text 2

LAURIE BAUER: *English Word-Formation*. Cambridge University Press 1983, pages 42–3

This extract traces the processes by which a new word or meaning enters the vocabulary of a language and becomes established. Whether or not the new term gains currency will depend on various factors, including the appearance of a new object or process which needs a name.

When a word first appears in a language, whether as a loan or as a nonce formation (i.e. a new complex word coined on the spur of the moment), it appears that speakers are aware of its newness, that is they are aware that they are exploiting the productivity of the language system. Thus, in modern journalistic language the word is often put in inverted commas, a phrase is added such as 'what has been called', 'as it is termed' and so on, or a complete gloss is provided. The large amount of written evidence for this awareness of novelty is a fairly recent phenomenon, since it is only in the twentieth century that vast numbers of dailies and periodicals have become commonplace, but it may be assumed that the awareness of innovation is not as recent as that, and that earlier generations put intonational 'inverted commas' round the term, and provided oral glosses in the same way. In literary language, where new forms are often produced specifically to provide effect, such marking does not take place, and the form is most frequently left to speak for itself; but it should be remembered that, statistically speaking, literary language is the exception rather than the rule in linguistic behaviour.

Whether or not the new term gains currency will depend upon a number of factors. One of these is the status of the person who used the term—Adams cites the example of *triphibian*, which may have been helped into currency by the fact that it was apparently first used by Winston Churchill—or, in journalistic terms, the status and circulation of the newspaper involved. But although this is a factor which is frequently mentioned, whether or not a word is accepted and used seems frequently to depend on the attitude to the word evinced by society as a whole. Society's stamp of approval in turn frequently depends on there being a need for the form in question. In the clearest cases this means that there is a new object or construct which needs a name (for example, *television, liquidizer*, and in linguistics such terms as *Chomsky adjunction* or *the category squish*), but frequently it is simply a matter of a known concept being required in a part of speech in which it has not previously been used.

In other cases there may not be an obvious need for a new word. For example, there is no obvious need for Danish *TV*, French *charter* and German *Fernsprecher*, given the prior existence of the synonymous forms *fjernsyn, affrété* and *Telephon*. In such cases, the new word may arise for reasons of prestige. In other cases, new complex words may be used to gain an effect, to save space (especially in newspaper headlines) or simply because the speaker cannot remember the usual lexeme used for the required concept. An example of the first of these is *dontopedology* 'putting one's foot in one's mouth', which has a humorous effect because it is a scientific-sounding label for something rather trivial; an example of the second is the recent use in headlines of *press freedom* in place of the more normal *freedom of the press*; and an example of the third (though one which may be gaining ground) is *equalitarian* for *egalitarian*. It would also be possible to speak of 'needs' in these instances, since in each case the existing list of lexemes fails to give immediate satisfaction in the speaker's search for an expression.

▷ *What conventions are used in spoken and written language to indicate that someone is aware of using a new word or meaning?*

▷ *An example of a word being used in a part of speech in which it has not previously been employed would be the term 'host' used as a verb in radio or television shows. Give further examples from broadcasting or another field.*

Text 3

ALAN CRUSE: *Meaning in Language. An Introduction to Semantics and Pragmatics*. Oxford University Press 1995, page 103

In this passage, the writer confronts the problem that the meanings we give to a word can vary considerably from one context to another. Sometimes the meanings are quite distinct, but sometimes there are subtle but still perceivable contrasts of meaning.

Once we try to grapple with the notion 'the meaning of a word', we come up against a serious problem: the interpretation we give to a particular word form can vary so greatly from context to context. The observable variations range from very gross, with little or no perceptible connection between the readings, as in: *They moored the boat to the bank* and *He is the manager of a local bank*, through clearly different but intuitively related readings, as in *My father's firm built this school* (*school* here refers to the building) and *John's school won the Football Charity Shield last year* (in this case *school* refers to (a subset of) the human population of the school), to relatively subtle variations, as in the case of *path* in *He was coming down the path to meet me even before I reached the garden gate* and *We followed a winding path through the woods* (a different mental image of a path is conjured up in the two cases), or *walk* in *Alice can walk already and she's only 11 months old* and *I usually walk to work*, where not only is the manner of walking different, but also are the implicit contrasts (in the first case, standing up unaided and talking and in the second case, driving or going by bus/train, etc.).

This type of variation, which is endemic in the vocabulary of any natural language, means that answers must be sought to questions like: Do words typically have multiple meanings?

How do we decide what constitutes 'a meaning'? Is there a finite number of such meanings? How are the meanings related to one another?

▷ *The examples of 'bank' show a clear separation of meanings. What is this called, and how can the separation be demonstrated?*

▷ *The differences in the meaning of 'school' have come about through applying a rule which derives one meaning ('people in a building') from another ('the building itself') on the basis of 'connection'. What is this process called? Provide further examples.*

Chapter 2
Word-formation

Text 4
DWIGHT BOLINGER and DONALD A. SEARS: *Aspects of Language* (3rd edn.) Harcourt Brace Jovanovich 1981, pages 59–60

Text 2 listed the conditions a coinage usually had to meet before entering the vocabulary. The present passage describes some of the word-formation processes that are involved, including some of the most irregular and bizarre.

We can analyse words, but once in a while the process is set in reverse and we create one, whether by accident or by design. The raw material generally conforms to the morphemes that can be discovered by analysing words that already exist—practically all words that are not imported bodily from some other language are made up of old words or modifications using standard affixes like *-ness* or *un-*. The less accidental the coinage the more respect it shows toward existing formative elements. This is especially true of scientific terms: *decompression, polystyrene, perosis, cacogenesis*—old morphemes are re-used in systematic ways. But no etymological pedigree is required. The coiner may mix elements of diverse origins—as in *monolingual*, half Greek and half Latin, or in *atonement*, with its two English words *at* and *one* tagged with a Latin suffix—or even carry over a whole phrase or sentence as in *touch-me-not*, *what-you-may-call-it*, or *IOU*. And a speaker may ignore the official roster and patch something up with splinters, as with *bumber*, altered from *umbr-* in *umbrella*, and *-shoot*, based on the *-chute* of *parachute*, that form the word *bumbershoot*. In between are fragments of all degrees of standardized efficiency and junkyard irregularity. *Hamburger* yields *-burger*, which is reattached in *nutburger*, *Gainesburger*, and *cheeseburger*. *Cafeteria* yields *-teria*, which is reattached in *carpeteria*, *groceteria*, and *washateria*. Trade names make easy use of almost any fragment, like the *-roni* of *macaroni* that is reattached in *Rice-a-Roni* and *Noodle-Roni*. Recently *alcoholic* has given part of itself to the creation of *workaholic*. The fabrication may re-use elements that have been re-used many times, or it may be a one-shot affair such as the punning reference to being a member of the *lowerarchy*, with *-archy* extracted from *hierarchy*. The principle is the same. The only thing a morpheme is good for is to be melted down and recast in a word.

The elements that are re-used most freely are called *productive*, the others *unproductive*, though both terms are relative. The suffix *-ate* is a Latinism that can hardly be used to make new words—but then some wag thinks up *discombobulate* and people accept it. At the other extreme the suffix *-er* looks as if we ought to be able to attach it to any verb and make a noun meaning 'one who performs the action': *worker*, *player*, *murderer*, *digger*, *eater*. Yet a glance at anomalies such as the following shows that we are less free than we think:

> They accused him–they were his accusers.
> *They blamed him–they were his blamers.
> They admire him–they are his admirers.
> *They loathe him–they are his loathers.
> She robs banks–she is a robber.
> *She steals things–she is a stealer.

These examples suggest why *-er* varies so in productivity. It is not that the language cannot *form* the noun *loather* but simply that we have no use for it. What retinue of people would it designate?

▷ The authors say here that 'once in a while' we create a new word 'whether by accident or design'. How do you think new words might be created by accident?

▷ One picturesque process is known as 'clipping'—the cutting away of one or more syllables from a word (e.g '-teria' from 'cafeteria'). What are the full words of which these are the clippings: 'decaf', 'fridge', 'memo', 'pram'?

Text 5

SIDNEY GREENBAUM: *The Oxford English Grammar*. Oxford University Press 1996, page 443

'Combining forms' (CFs) have certain features in common with the affixes used to form derivatives and compounds. Like prefixes they occur before (and like suffixes after) another element to form a word (e.g. 'Euro + sceptic', 'futur + ology'). Moreover, two CFs can come together to form a word ('bibliography') just as two simple words can be joined to form a compound ('headache').

Straddling affixation and compounding are processes involving combining forms. Combining forms are segments that do not occur as separate words in the language and like affixes they are attached before or after another segment to constitute a word. They are usually neo-classical; that is to say, they are mostly segments originating from Latin and Greek that are used to form words in English. Examples of initial combining forms are *Anglo-, astro-, bio-, electro-, Euro-, psycho-, tele-*; examples of final combining forms are *-cide, -cracy, -gram, -graph, -logy, -phile, -phobe*. These may be combined with established English words: *biochemistry, electromagnetism, psychotherapy, Eurosceptic, teleconference, meritocracy, futurology, escapologist*. In this way, elements from the classical languages enjoy a new life in English, forming words that did not exist in the original languages. Apart from their use in non-specialized language, combining forms are a common feature of scientific terminology, particularly in chemistry and pharmacology.

Initial combining forms generally end in a vowel, mostly *o*, though other vowels are also found, e.g. *agriculture, docudrama*.

When a new initial combining form is created, it tends to end in *o*. It may be shortened for that purpose from a longer word: *eco-*, from *ecology* and *ecological*, provides the first segment of *ecosystem* and *ecocentric*, *Euro-*, from *Europe* and *European*, yields *Eurocrat* and *Eurospeak*. If that possibility is not available, the combining vowel *o* is added to convert the first segment into a combining form, as in *speedometer*, *futurology*, *meritocracy*, *Francophone*.

Combining forms resemble affixes in being initial or final segments of words. However, two combining forms can be joined to form a word (*psychology*, *homophobe*, *Eurocrat*, *astronaut*), just as two bases can be conjoined in a compound word, whereas it is not possible to have a word consisting of just a prefix and a suffix. Indeed, final combining forms regularly combine only with initial combining forms: *-logy*, for example, requires an initial combining form such as *psycho-*, *socio-*, *anthropo-*, *futuro-*, *escapo-*. Hence, *pigeoncide* (attested in a news item in the British daily *The Independent*, 2 January 1991, p. 1) is irregular, though intelligible, as would be *spacenaut* in place of *astronaut*.

▷ *The author points out that CFs are widely used to form scientific terms. Give examples of these using the initial CFs 'electro-' and 'psycho-', and the final CFs '-graph' and '-logy'.*

▷ *What is meant by saying that, through the use of CFs, 'elements from the classical languages enjoy a new life in English'?*

Text 6

P.H. MATTHEWS: *Morphology* (2nd edn.) Cambridge University Press 1991, pages 94–5

The writer of this excerpt asks how we can distinguish, in terms of meaning and form, between compounds and syntactic constructions. The difficulty is that it is often hard to find a set of criteria all of which point in the same direction.

Policeman and *postman* originate, at least, in compounds with the second member *man*. But phonetically they have lost the full vowel: [pə'liːsmən] not -[mæn]. Moreover, there is another class of forms which do have [mæn], such as *insurance man* or (in my speech) *gas man*. Has the -[mən] then broken away from *man*, becoming a lexical formative on its own? There are two possible objections. Firstly, the Plural (also [mən]) would be slightly puzzling. As a reduced form of *men* it is what one expects; but if it has no synchronic connection with *men*, why do we not find regular Plurals ('*policemans*', etc.) beginning to develop? One might hear such forms from children (along with *singed* for *sang* and other hyper-regularities), but they do not become established. The second and more important objection lies in the opposition between *policeman* and *policewoman*. In meaning, one is to the other as *man* is to *woman*, and the latter is a more recent form which takes the former as a model. Nor would *postwoman* be unexpected, provided that 'postwomen' existed. The form in -*woman* suggests that those in -[mən] also retain their character as compounds. But the case has to be argued.

In a language such as English there are also serious problems in determining the boundary between compounds and syntactic constructions. The definition itself is clear: a compound (such as *madman*) is 'one word', and a construction (such as [*a*] *mad man*) two or more separate 'words'. But in practice what are the criteria for distinguishing them? 'Girl-friend', for example, could be written in any of three ways: as two words (*girl friend*), as one word hyphenated (*girl-friend*), or unhyphenated. We have used other examples, like *fish farm* or *safety pin*, which are usually, if not always, written as two words. Clearly, we cannot take the spelling conventions as our guide. Any printer or typist knows that they are not consistent. But by what criterion have we in fact decided that these and other forms are one lexeme and not two? Criteria may be sought at every level: from morphology and semantics, from phonology and syntax. Where a morphological criterion is available it may, of course, be decisive. *Socio-economic* is certainly a compound, because its first member is a stem or stem-variant plus suffix (compare *social*, *soci-o-logy*, etc.) which cannot form a word on its own. The same is true of the type *Anglo-American*, *Franco-Chinese*, *Italo-Celtic*, etc. On the other hand, *heir apparent* is not a compound, because in the Plural (*heirs apparent*) *heir* is still inflected as a separate unit. Such tests are largely sufficient in languages where most words are inflected. Take, for example, the Latin Verb *liquefacio* 'make liquid'. This has a compound stem whose first member, *lique*, is in turn a bare stem of the simple *liquet* 'be liquid'. *benedico* ('bless' in Church Latin) is a compound whose first member is the Adverb *bene* 'well'. This cannot be replaced by its Comparative or Superlative (say, *optimedico* 'bless especially'). But in English there is generally no positive test. *Social Democratic* may be a compound, in that *Social* is not inflected separately; but then how could it be? Equally, it may NOT be a compound, in that *Social* can appear independently; but then so can *mad* in *madman*, *girl* in *girlfriend* and so on. The types which do allow positive results (*socio-economic* or *heir apparent*) are only the extreme cases. The test for *heir apparent* will also reveal uncertainties. In *solicitor general*, the first member is not usually inflected (e.g. *the solicitor generals in the last three governments*). But perhaps a pedant will insist that it should be, and there are certainly styles in which *solicitors general* would be more normal. Turning to a more ordinary situation, could three people in a restaurant order *three prunes and custards* or *three tournedo Rossini's*? For the author, at least, both are more acceptable than *three apple-pie and creams* or *three sole bonne-femme's*. There are several factors at work, and it is not easy to be sure of the facts.

Semantic criteria have often been emphasized. The phrases *a black bird* and *a blue jay* have meanings predictable from the individual words and their construction: the former refers to any 'bird' which is 'black' (e.g. a rook), and the latter to a 'jay' which is 'blue' (whatever that means, a European reader may say!). But the compounds *blackbird* and *bluejay* have meanings which are not predictable; the latter too is the name of a particular (North American) species.

▷ *Consider 'soup spoon' and 'tea spoon'. It is easy to work out their meanings from those of their components. Yet, despite their 'transparency' they are often referred to as compounds, and both appear in various dictionaries. How can this be explained?*

▷ *The author cites 'three prunes and custards' (with final '-s') as an indication that the whole expression is inflected, 'prunes and custard' by this criterion being a compound. But isn't the meaning of the whole predictable from the meanings of the individual words?*

Chapter 3
Multiple meaning

Text 7

MURRAY KNOWLES and ROSAMUND MOON: *Introducing Metaphor*. Routledge 2005, pages 4–6

Metaphor is a basic process in the development of lexical items and their meanings. Many meanings of polysemous words are metaphors, and many idioms originate as metaphors. Moreover, we may use metaphors to explain more precisely what a thing is like, or to convey what we feel about it.

Metaphor is pervasive in language, and there are two principal ways in which it is important.

First, in relation to individual words: metaphor is a basic process in the formation of words and word meanings. Concepts and meanings are lexicalized, or expressed in words, through metaphor. Many senses of multi-sense words are metaphors of different kinds, as in the meanings of *field*, *hurt*, and *dark* in the following Bank of English (BoE) examples:

She has published extensively in the **field** of psychology.
The failure has **hurt** him deeply.
… the end of a long tale, full of **dark** hints and unspeakable innuendos.

Similarly, the names of many new concepts or devices are metaphorical or extended uses of pre-existing words: for example, computer terms such as *web*, *bug*, and *virus*. Many compound words encapsulate metaphors: *browbeat*, *foothill*, *pigeonhole*. Idioms and proverbs are often metaphorical in origin: *don't put all your eggs in one basket*, *miss the boat*, *rattle someone's cage*, and, more obscurely, *kick the bucket* and *a red herring*. These are mainly conventional metaphors.

Second, in relation to discourse: metaphor is important because of its functions—explaining, clarifying, describing, expressing, evaluating, entertaining. There are many reasons *why* we use metaphors in speech or writing: not least, because there is sometimes no other word to refer to a particular thing. But where we have a choice, we choose metaphors in order to communicate what we think or how we feel about something; to explain what a particular thing is like; to convey a meaning in a more interesting or creative way; or to do all of these. We will look at examples later. Significantly, a lot of our understanding of things is mediated through metaphor. That is, we might well not understand them except with the help of metaphorical models or analogies, and our understanding is itself conditioned by the metaphor. For example, the cells in our bodies react biologically in complex ways to infection: we can understand the process more easily through a metaphor of war, thinking of it in terms of fighting and invasion, as in

> Scientists believe stress may suppress development of T-cells, the white blood cells which help to **fight off invading** micro-organisms. (BoE)

Other metaphors might have been used, but this is the dominant, most familiar one, and the way in which we now conceptualize the biological process is determined by it. Similarly with the example *throughout the whole range*, from earlier in this chapter: we represent diversity as physical space. It is typical that metaphors use concrete images to convey something abstract, helping to communicate what is hard to explain.

▷ *What is meant by calling the idioms 'miss the boat' and 'rattle someone's cage' 'conventional' metaphors? What term would you use to describe metaphors that are the opposite of conventional? Give examples.*

▷ *The authors suggest that it is quite common to use concrete images to convey abstract concepts. How is the concept of 'imagination' represented by being associated with specific verbs, as follows: 'capture the imagination', 'grip the imagination', 'grasp the imagination'?*

Text 8

GEORGE LAKOFF: 'The contemporary theory of metaphor' in Andrew Ortony (ed.): *Metaphor and Thought* (2nd edn.) Cambridge University Press 1993, pages 206–7

English has many uncreative, everyday phrases describing love as stages on a journey. To find a general principle explaining how these phrases about journeys are used to characterize love, the writer invokes a metaphorical scenario. One domain of experience, love, is being explained, metaphorically, in terms of a different domain of experience, a journey.

Imagine a love relationship described as follows:

Our relationship has hit a *dead-end street*.

Here love is being conceptualized as a journey, with the implication that the relationship is *stalled*, that the lovers cannot *keep going the way they've been going*, that they must *turn back*, or abandon the relationship altogether. This is not an isolated case. English has many everyday expressions that are based on a conceptualization of love as a journey, and they are used not just for talking about love, but for reasoning about it as well. Some are necessarily about love; others can be understood that way:

Look *how far we've come*. It's been *a long*, *bumpy road*. We can't *turn back* now. We're at a *crossroads*. We may have to *go our separate ways*. The relationship isn't *going anywhere*. We're *spinning our wheels*. Our relationship is *off the track*. The marriage is *on the rocks*. We may have to *bail out* of this relationship.

These are ordinary, everyday English expressions. They are not poetic, nor are they necessarily used for special rhetorical effect. Those like *look how far we've come*, which aren't necessarily about love, can readily be understood as being about love.

As a linguist and a cognitive scientist, I ask two commonplace questions:

- Is there a general principle governing how these linguistic expressions about journeys are used to characterize love?
- Is there a general principle governing how our patterns of inference about journeys are used to reason about love when expressions such as these are used?

The answer to both is yes. Indeed, there is a single general principle that answers both questions, but it is a general principle that is neither part of the grammar of English, nor the English lexicon. Rather, it is part of the conceptual system underlying English. It is a principle for understanding the domain of love in terms of the domain of journeys.

The principle can be stated informally as a metaphorical scenario:

> The lovers are travelers on a journey together, with their common life goals seen as destinations to be reached. The relationship is their vehicle, and it allows them to pursue those common goals together. The relationship is seen as fulfilling its purpose as long as it allows them to make progress toward their common goals. The journey isn't easy. There are impediments, and there are places (crossroads) where a decision has to be made about which direction to go in and whether to keep traveling together.

The metaphor involves understanding one domain of experience, love, in terms of a very different domain of experience, journeys. More technically, the metaphor can be understood as a mapping (in the mathematical sense) from a source domain (in this case, journeys) to a target domain (in this case, love). The mapping is tightly structured. There are ontological correspondences, according to which entities in the domain of love (e.g., the lovers, their common goals, their difficulties, the love relationship, etc.) correspond systematically to entities in the domain of a journey (the travelers, the vehicle, destinations, etc.).

To make it easier to remember what mappings there are in the conceptual system, Johnson and I adopted a strategy for naming such mappings, using mnemonics which suggest the mapping. Mnemonic names typically (though not always) have the form: target-domain is source-domain, or alternatively, target-domain as source-domain. In this case, the name of the mapping is love is a journey. When I speak of the *love is a journey* metaphor, I am using a mnemonic for a set of ontological correspondences that characterize a mapping, namely:

The love-as-journey mapping
The lovers correspond to travelers.
The love relationship corresponds to the vehicle.
The lovers' common goals correspond to their common des-
tinations on the journey.

Difficulties in the relationship correspond to impediments to
travel. It is a common mistake to confuse the name of the mapping, *love is a journey*, for the mapping itself. The mapping is the
set of correspondences. Thus, whenever I refer to a metaphor by
a mnemonic like *love is a journey*, I will be referring to such a set
of correspondences.

▷ *Which of the expressions quoted in the first four paragraphs*
are necessarily about love and which could be understood in
that way?

▷ *The author stresses that he is talking about ordinary, everyday*
expressions, not phrases used creatively or for special effect.
What does this tell us about the approach to metaphor being
presented here?

Text 9

STEPHEN ULLMANN: *Semantics: An Introduction to the*
Science of Meaning. Blackwell 1962, pages 161–2

We often find, when speaking in a specialized context, that
there are some meanings which are so clearly implied that
there is no need to spell them out. Take 'race meeting', and
'court action'. Professionals in these spheres see no need for a
modifying word; they simply say 'meeting' or 'action'. Later,
either of these general words may acquire other specialized
senses, only one of which will be applicable in any given
situation.

Specialization in a social milieu.—Michel Bréal drew attention
to the fact that polysemy often arises through a kind of verbal
shorthand. 'In every situation, in every trade or profession', he
wrote, 'there is a certain idea which is so much present to one's
mind, so clearly implied, that it seems unnecessary to state it
when speaking'. For a lawyer, *action* will naturally mean 'legal

action'; for the soldier it will mean a military operation, without any need for a qualifying epithet. In this way the same word may acquire a number of specialized senses only one of which will be applicable in a given milieu. We have already seen an example of this process in the polysemy of the word *style*. Similarly, *paper* can refer not only to the material in general but to a variety of other things: legal or official documents; a newspaper; a set of examination questions; a communication read or sent to a learned society; in the plural it can also denote identity documents; certificates accompanying the resignation of an officer; documents showing the ownership, nationality and destination of a ship, etc. In the past there were also some other specialized uses; the word could mean, for example, a note fastened on the back of a criminal, specifying his offence:

> Methinks I should not thus be led along,
> Mail'd up in shame, with *papers* on my back.
> *King Henry the Sixth, Part Two*, Act II, scene 4.

One could indefinitely multiply examples of words which have a general meaning in ordinary language and specialized senses in more restricted spheres: *company, interest, security, share* in commerce; *overture, key, score* in music; *signature* in music and printing; *stage, pit, curtain* in the theatre; *screen* in the cinema; *broadcasting* in radio; *viewing* in television; *score, goal, back, centre, bat, century* in various sports, to mention only a few.

The extreme form of specialization is reached when a common noun virtually becomes a proper name denoting a single object in a particular environment. This has happened in the case of some famous London districts and landmarks: the *City*, the *House*, the *Abbey*, the *Tower*, the *Yard*. The name *Provence* is the regular French continuation of the Latin *provincia*, as if that region were the province *par excellence*; the ordinary French word, *province*, which has been taken over into English, is a learned borrowing from Latin.

▷ *What other meanings of 'action' appear to have developed in a specialized milieu?*

▷ *In the case of 'City', 'House', etc., a common noun has become a proper noun referring to a single place. Which of the names*

listed in the text have taken the further step of denoting the
people who regularly work in the places in question?

Chapter 4
Meaningful relations

Text 10
FRANK PALMER: *Semantics: A New Outline* (2nd edn.)
Cambridge University Press 1981, pages 85–6

In this account of hyponymy we are shown that 'tulip'
and 'rose', as co-hyponyms, are included in 'flower', as
superordinate. There is not, however, always a superordinate,
and in other arrangements involving hyponyms the same
word (in different meanings) may appear more than once. In
one sense, 'animal' may contrast with 'vegetable'; in another
it can contrast with 'bird', 'fish', and 'insect'.

Hyponymy involves us in the notion of inclusion in the sense
that *tulip* and *rose* are included in *flower*, and *lion* and *elephant*
in *mammal* (or perhaps *animal*—see below). Similarly *scarlet* is
included in *red*. Inclusion is thus a matter of class membership.
The 'upper' term is the superordinate and the 'lower' term the
hyponym.

Here we are concerned with members of a class, with, that
is to say, co-hyponyms. Yet oddly there is not always a superordinate term. Lyons observed that in Classical Greek there is a
superordinate term to cover a variety of professions and crafts,
'carpenter', 'doctor', 'flute player', 'helmsman', 'shoemaker',
etc., but none in English. The nearest possible term is *craftsman*,
but that would not include *doctor*, *flute player* or *helmsman*.
Similarly, and rather strangely, there is no superordinate term for
all colour words, *red*, *blue*, *green*, *white*, etc.; the term *coloured*
usually excludes *black* and *white* (and *grey* too), or else (used to
refer to race), means 'non-white'.

The same term may appear in several places in the hierarchy.
This is, of course, possible only if it is polysemic (has several
meanings); in one of its meanings it may actually be superordinate to itself in another meaning (though we should usually

avoid using both terms in the same context). Thus *animal* may be used (1) in contrast with *vegetable* to include birds, fishes, insects as well as mammals, (2) in the sense of 'mammal' to contrast with birds, fishes and insects, to include both humans and beasts, (3) in the sense of 'beast' to contrast with *human*. Thus it occurs three times in the hierarchical classification of nature. Figure 1 illustrates the point clearly:

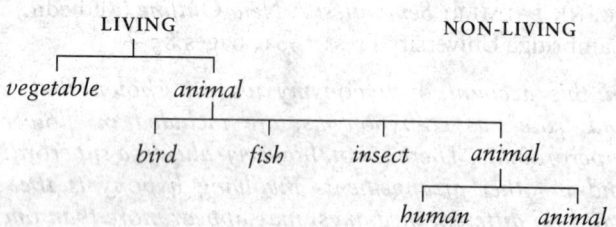

FIGURE 1

There is a similar situation with the word *dog*. The word *sheep* is used for all creatures of a certain species; it is the superordinate term of *ewe*, *lamb*, *ram*, etc. There are similar terms *pig* for *sow*, *boar*, *piglet* and *horse* for *stallion*, *mare*, *colt*, etc. But the superordinate term for dogs is *dog*, though *dog* is also the hyponym as distinct from *bitch*. Figure 2 will help. We can, of course, avoid the ambiguity of *dog* by using the term *male*; *male dog* would be the hyponym to contrast with *bitch*. We can also form hyponymous sets where no single-word hyponyms exist in English in a similar way, e.g. *giraffe*, *male giraffe*, *female giraffe*, *baby giraffe*.

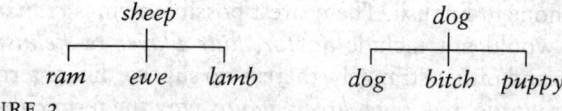

FIGURE 2

▷ *It is not rare to find a set phrase or compound functioning as the co-hyponym of a simple word (cf. 'yam', 'sweet potato'). Provide further examples, drawing on plant and flower names.*

▷ *A hyponym of one word may be the superordinate of another (cf. 'vegetable', 'tuber', 'potato'). Give further examples.*

ALAN CRUSE: *Lexical Semantics*. Cambridge University
Press 1986, page 169

*In this chapter, the author describes two ways of dividing
the human body. It can first be divided into parts such as the
trunk, the head, and the arms, called 'segmental parts'. Parts
of the second type, called 'systemic parts' include the skeleton,
muscles, and nerves.*

Consider the ways of dividing the human body. We can either
divide it into parts such as *trunk*, *head*, *limbs*, etc., or we can
equally validly divide it in quite another way, into *skeleton*,
muscles, *nerves*, *blood vessels*, etc. Parts of the first type have
a greater degree of spatial cohesiveness, and presumably, also,
perceptual salience (when viewed from the outside, at any rate).
They will be called 'segmental parts'; as we traverse a whole
along its major spatial axes, we typically encounter the segmental parts sequentially. Parts of the second type have a greater
functional unity, a greater consistency of internal constitution,
but they are spatially inter-penetrating, running along the major
axes of the body. These will be termed 'systemic parts'. Each of
these principles of division is as valid as the other, but it seems
that ordinary language has a preference for segmental parts.
Many wholes can be partitioned in ways parallel to the human
body. A *house*, for instance, may be divided into *living-room*,
dining-room, *kitchen*, *hall*, *bedrooms*, *cellar*, *loft*, etc. (segmental parts); or *brickwork*, *joinery*, *plasterwork*, *plumbing*, *wir-
ing*, etc. (systemic parts—notice that these are quasi-meronyms
of *house*, because they are mass nouns, whereas *house* is a count
noun). The case of *house* (and other buildings) is further complicated by the fact that the segmental parts can be seen either
in terms of spaces (e.g. rooms), or in terms of the structural elements which define those spaces (for instance, the *walls*, *floors*
and *ceilings* are also parts of a *house*). Whatever type of division
is adopted for a particular hierarchy, it must remain constant
throughout the structure.

▷ *The author states that 'ordinary language has a preference
for segmental parts'. What does he mean by this?*

> The systemic parts listed for 'houses' in the passage include 'brickwork', 'joinery', and 'plasterwork'. But these are arguably a range of materials from which the house is made. If you wished to establish a closer parallel between muscles, nerves, veins, etc., in the human body, and systemic parts in a house, what words would you suggest for the latter?

Chapter 5
Set phrases

Text 12

ROSAMUND MOON: *Fixed Expressions and Idioms in English. A Corpus-Based Approach*. Clarendon Press 1998, pages 131–2

This passage deals with 'truncation', a process by which a longer expression is reduced from its original full form to a grammatically shorter one. A truncated form can evoke the complete expression, with its original meaning, but at the same time may come to have an independent life of its own.

Amplification and truncation are two sides of the same coin, but in the majority of cases listed below, the fuller versions are fairly clearly attested as the original forms. Many are traditional proverbs and sayings, downgraded from their canonical or earliest forms to lower-level grammatical units: a compound sentence to a single clause, or a clause to a group:

    a bird in the hand (is worth two in the bush)
    birds of a feather (flock together)
    don't count one's chickens (before they're hatched)
    he who pays the piper calls the tune, call the tune
    let the cobbler stick to his last, stick to one's last
    make hay (while the sun shines)
    (sow the wind and) reap the whirlwind

The reduced forms can be seen in terms of ellipsis, since in many cases an allusion to the original and fuller form remains. However, they are institutionalized, and many can be regarded as lexical items in their own right. *A rolling stone gathers no moss* is complicated in that both the nominal *rolling stone* and the verb phrase *gather moss* are institutionalized as individual items. In

a drowning man will clutch at a straw
clutch/grasp at straws

it's the (last) straw that breaks the camel's back
the last straw/final straw

the truncated forms themselves have variations. In a few cases, the original fuller form has almost disappeared from the lexicon:

Finders keepers (losers weepers)
happy the bride that the sun shines on (and blessed are the
    dead that the rain falls on)
(speech is silver but) silence is golden
butter wouldn't melt in her mouth (but cheese wouldn't
    choke her)

In the above cases, the reduced forms have become fossilized as the canonical forms. Truncation can also occur on an ad hoc basis:

My mother was hysterical and my father called me a lot of unpleasant names. I stood it for a bit and then I'm afraid I said to him that **what was sauce for the goose** and at least I wasn't married. (OHPC: fiction)

In one audacious move, D & B sent a questionnaire to Geoff Croughton, secretary of the Bank of England. After all, **nothing ventured** and all that. (OHPC: journalism)

▷ *It may be more common, especially in informal English, to use the truncated rather than the full forms. Suggest reasons for this.*

▷ *Various reduced forms are described as being 'institutionalized'. What does this mean?*

Text 13
SYLVIANE GRANGER: 'Prefabricated patterns in advanced EFL writing: collocations and formulae' in A.P. Cowie (ed.): *Phraseology: Theory, Analysis, and Applications*. Clarendon Press 1998, pages 152–3

Two groups of informants, one made up of native speakers, the other of non-natives, were asked to choose what for them were the acceptable adjective collocates of 11 amplifiers (i.e. of words such as 'wholly'). They were also asked to mark any adjective that collocated more frequently than all the others. The foreign learners marked far fewer collocations than natives, failing to recognize such collocations as 'bitterly cold' and 'readily available'.

We have established that learners are using collocations, but that they underuse native-like collocations and use atypical word-combinations. The results of an independent study I carried out suggest that this is probably due to an underdeveloped sense of salience and of what constitutes a significant collocation. The aim of this study was to extract introspective data on collocations and involved submitting a word-combination test to 112 informants, 56 French learners of English and 56 native-speakers of English.[1] Informants were asked to choose, from a list of 15 adjectives in each case, the acceptable collocates of 11 amplifiers, by circling all the adjectives which in their opinion collocated with the amplifier. If they were unsure about a particular adjective, they were instructed to underline it and if they felt that one adjective was more frequently associated with the amplifier than all the others, they were requested to mark it with an asterisk.

It was the comparison of the forms marked with an asterisk by the learners and the natives, and which therefore indicated those combinations which were particularly salient in the subjects' minds, that yielded particularly interesting results. All in all, the learners marked with an asterisk over 100 fewer combinations than the natives (280 vs. 384). Table 1 gives clear evidence of the learners' weak sense of salience. *Readily available*, for instance, was asterisked by 43 native speakers but by a mere 8 learners. *Bitterly cold* was selected by 40 native speakers but only 7 learners. For *blissfully*, the native speaker selections were evenly distributed between *blissfully happy* and *blissfully ignorant*, asterisked by 19 and 20 informants respectively, while not one single learner marked the latter combination and only 4 selected the former.

Amplifiers	Native-speaker responses	Learner responses
readily	*readily available* (43)	*readily available* (8)
bitterly	*bitterly cold* (40)	*bitterly cold* (7)
		bitterly aware (3)
		bitterly miserable (2)
blissfully	*blissfully happy* (19)	*blissfully happy* (4)
	blissfully ignorant (20)	
fully	*fully aware* (33)	*fully aware* (21)
	fully reliable (3)	*fully reliable* (15)
		fully different (6)
		fully significant (5)
		fully impossible (3)
		fully available (2)
highly	*highly significant* (33)	*highly significant* (15)
	highly reliable (3)	*highly reliable* (7)
	highly important (2)	*highly important* (6)
	highly aware (3)	*highly impossible* (6)
		highly difficult (5)
		highly essential (4)
		highly different (2)

TABLE 1 *Native-speaker and learner responses to word-combining test*

On balance, the learners marked a greater number of types of combinations than the natives, indicating that the learners' sense of salience is not only weak, but also partly misguided. Although there was evidence of a good sense of salience among a significant number of learners for some combinations, such as *fully aware*, and *fully reliable*, the learners also considered four other combinations to be significant collocations, none of which was selected by the native speakers, thus: *fully different/significant/impossible/available*. Besides selecting *highly significant*, learners also marked six other combinations with *highly*, four of which were not marked by native speakers. In fact, *highly impossible/difficult/essential/different* were together selected more often than *highly significant*. This is somewhat paradoxical when considered in the light of evidence that learners underuse *highly* in their writing, but this could perhaps be put down to the production reception distinction.

[1] The eleven amplifiers presented were: *highly, seriously, readily, blissfully, vitally, fully, perfectly, heavily, bitterly, absolutely, utterly*. The format of the test was as follows:

readily significant reliable ill different essential aware miserable available clear happy difficult ignorant impossible cold important.

bitterly significant reliable ill different essential aware miserable available clear happy difficult ignorant impossible cold important.

▷ *Using the lists of amplifiers and adjectives set out in the footnotes and the instructions provided in the passage, repeat the experiment for yourself. Compare your results with those given in the table.*

▷ *The term 'sense of salience' is used in the passage but not defined. Provide a definition.*

Text 14

JOHN SINCLAIR: *Corpus, Concordance, Collocation.*
Oxford University Press 1991, pages 110–2

The author argues that there is too much freedom of choice in a model of language which regards a text as a series of slots which have to be filled, with almost any word being able to fill each place. The 'idiom principle', by contrast, assumes that a speaker has available many partly ready-made phrases. These represent single choices, even though it may seem possible to analyse them into smaller elements.

It is clear that words do not occur at random in a text, and that the open-choice principle does not provide for substantial enough restraints on consecutive choices. We would not produce normal text simply by operating the open-choice principle.

To some extent, the nature of the world around us is reflected in the organization of language and contributes to the unrandomness. Things which occur physically together have a stronger chance of being mentioned together; also concepts in the same philosophical area, and the results of exercising a number of organizing features such as contrasts or series. But even allowing for these, there are many ways of saying things, many choices within language that have little or nothing to do with the world outside.

There are sets of linguistic choices which come under the heading of register, and which can be seen as large-scale conditioning choices. Once a register choice is made, and these are normally social choices, then all the slot-by-slot choices are massively reduced in scope or even, in some cases, pre-empted.

Allowing for register as well, there is still far too much opportunity for choice in the model, and the principle of idiom is put forward to account for the restraints that are not captured by the open-choice model.

The principle of idiom is that a language user has available to him or her a large number of semi-preconstructed phrases that constitute single choices, even though they might appear to be analysable into segments. To some extent, this may reflect the recurrence of similar situations in human affairs; it may illustrate a natural tendency to economy of effort; or it may be motivated in part by the exigencies of real-time conversation. However it arises, it has been relegated to an inferior position in most current linguistics, because it does not fit the open-choice model.

At its simplest, the principle of idiom can be seen in the apparently simultaneous choice of two words, for example, *of course*. This phrase operates effectively as a single word, and the word space, which is structurally bogus, may disappear in time, as we see in *maybe, anyway*, and *another*.

Where there is no variation in the phrase, we are dealing with a fairly trivial mismatch between the writing system and the grammar. The *of* in *of course* is not the preposition *of* that is found in grammar books. The preposition *of* is normally found after the noun head of a nominal group, or in a quantifier like *a pint of* ... In an open-choice model, *of* can be followed by any nominal group. Similarly, *course* is not the countable noun that dictionaries mention; its meaning is not a property of the word, but of the phrase. If it were a countable noun in the singular it would have to be preceded by a determiner to be grammatical, so it clearly is not.

It would be reasonable to add phrases like *of course* to the list of compounds, like *cupboard*, whose elements have lost their semantic identity, and make allowance for the intrusive word space. The same treatment could be given to hundreds of similar phrases—any occasion where one decision leads to more than one word in text. Idioms, proverbs, clichés, technical terms, jargon expressions, phrasal verbs, and the like could all be covered by a fairly simple statement.

However, the principle of idiom is far more pervasive and elusive than we have allowed so far. It has been noted by many writers on language, but its importance has been largely neglected. Some features of the idiom principle follow:

a Many phrases have an indeterminate extent. As an example, consider *set eyes on*. This seems to attract a pronoun subject, and either *never* or a temporal conjunction like *the moment*, *the first time*, and the word *has* as an auxiliary to *set*. How much of this is integral to the phrase, and how much is in the nature of collocational attraction?

b Many phrases allow internal lexical variation. For example, there seems to be little to choose between *in some cases* and *in some instances*; or between *set x on fire* and *set fire to x*.

c Many phrases allow internal lexical syntactic variation. Consider the phrase *it's not in his nature to ...* The word *it* is part of the phrase, and so is the verb *is*—though this verb can vary to *was* and perhaps can include modals. *Not* can be replaced by any 'broad' negative, including *hardly*, *scarcely*, etc. *In* is fixed, but *his* can be replaced by any possessive pronoun and perhaps by some names with *'s*. *Nature* is fixed.

d Many phrases allow some variation in word order. Continuing the last example, we can postulate *to recriminate is not in his nature*, or *it is not in the nature of an academic to ...*

e Many uses of words and phrases attract other words in strong collocation; for example, *hard work*, *hard luck*, *hard facts*, *hard evidence*.

f Many uses of words and phrases show a tendency to co-occur with certain grammatical choices. For example, it has been pointed out that the phrasal verb *set about*, in its meaning of something like 'inaugurate', is closely associated with a following verb in the *-ing* form, for example, *set about leaving*... What is more, the second verb is usually transitive, for example, *set about testing it*. Very often, *set* will be found in co-occurrence patterns.

g Many uses of words and phrases show a tendency to occur in a certain semantic environment. For example, the verb *happen* is associated with unpleasant things—accidents and the like.

The overwhelming nature of this evidence leads us to elevate the principle of idiom from being a rather minor feature, compared with grammar, to being at least as important as grammar in the explanation of how meaning arises in text.

▷ *The idiomatic character of some phrasal verbs (e.g. 'give up') ties in with the choice of a following verb in the '–ing' form. What other evidence does the extract provide of grammatical and lexical choices interacting with each other?*

▷ *Note the suggestion that 'happen' is associated with unpleasant things. Is this true of all the dictionary meanings of the verb?*

Chapter 6
Components of meaning

Text 15

EUGENE NIDA: *Componential Analysis of Meaning.* Mouton 1975, pages 72–3

The author refers to the 'supplementary' components of meaning which, over time, become associated with the names of different kinds of seats. Different problems are involved when we wish to extend a componential analysis of the kind seen in Chapter 6 to include more types of seat. The term 'seat' itself poses special problems because it has a general, inclusive meaning but also denotes an item of furniture normally fixed to the floor.

Because of the various settings (both practical and linguistic) in which the terms *chair, bench, stool*, and *hassock* and their corresponding referents occur, certain supplementary components become associated with these terms. *Chair*, which refers to the most common object for sitting, has the least distinctive supplementary components. In fact, for most persons there are few if any such features. But for *bench* there is a supplementary component of something relatively uncomfortable, both physically and socially. *Stool*, on the other hand, suggests either conviviality, if the context is a bar, or something quite lowly and/or distinctly utilitarian, if the context is one of a barn or workshop. For *hassock* the supplementary components involve informality of setting and relaxed atmosphere. These supplementary components are not to be confused with the emotive associations with these terms. For the most part, these terms are relatively neutral with regard to emotive meanings, except, for example, where *stool* may trigger for some persons a series of associations with being inebriated and *hassock* may have a strong carry-over from its use in designating a prayer stool—something small boys often learn to loathe.

Though the componential analysis of the meanings of *chair, bench, stool*, and *hassock* seems quite straightforward, despite certain matters of indeterminacy, the problems become somewhat more complex if one adds a few terms to this basic set, e.g. *seat, sofa, love seat, davenport*, and *pew*. These are also pieces of furniture, designed, primarily for sitting, but they introduce several other contrastive features. *Sofa, love seat*, and *davenport* all differ from *bench* in that they are upholstered and have a back and normally have arms. But a *love seat* is designed for only two persons and a *sofa* and *davenport* are designed for two or more. *Sofa* and *davenport* differ primarily in that the latter is usually somewhat longer and may be used for sleeping. A *pew* shares with *bench* the feature of being designed for several persons, but it normally has a back and is rarely upholstered, even though it may have cushions.

The term *seat*, however, involves special difficulties, largely because it has two different meanings. It may refer to a place on *chairs, stools, sofas*, etc., as when a hostess may say to a guest, *Do have a seat!* In this sense, the meaning of *seat* belongs to the domain of terms such as *place*, *location*, *position*, and *space*. But *seat* is also used to designate particular objects for sitting, e.g. *they removed the first row of seats in the tourist section* and *this seat does not recline properly*. This second meaning of *seat* is closely related to that of *chair*, that is, an object for sitting, designed for one person, and having a back and legs; but it differs from *chair* in referring to an object having a fixed position; that is to say, it is not easily or normally moved about. There is, however, one point of indeterminacy in this usage, namely, the box seats at a theater. One buys so many box seats, but the actual objects may be called chairs or seats; usually they are called chairs if they are movable and seats if they are not movable, but the usage may vary. Such alternation is not strange, however, for alternation of usage is found at all levels of language, especially in instances in which there are conflicting analogical pressures. And this is pre-cisely what exists in the case of *chair* vs. *seat* in speaking of the furniture to be found in theater boxes.

▷ *What particular problems are posed by the definition of 'hassock'?*

▷ *Identify from the passage the defining features of a 'love seat'. Has any essential feature been omitted?*

Text 16
GEOFFREY LEECH: *Semantics. The Study of Meaning* (2nd edn.) Penguin 1981, pages 14–5

'Social' meaning is the meaning which a piece of language conveys about the social circumstances of its use. This many-sided aspect of meaning is 'decoded' by identifying different stylistic levels within English.

We turn now to two aspects of communication which have to do with the situation in which an utterance takes place. Social Meaning is that which a piece of language conveys about the social circumstances of its use. In part, we 'decode' the social meaning of a text through our recognition of different dimen-sions and levels of style within the same language. We recognize some words or pronunciations as being dialectal, i.e. as telling us something of the geographical or social origin of the speaker: other features of language tell us something of the social relationship between the speaker and hearer: we have a scale of 'status' usage, for example, descending from formal and literary English at one end to colloquial, familiar, and eventually slang English at the other.

One account has recognized, among others, the following dimensions of socio-stylistic variation (I have added examples of the categories of usage one would distinguish on each dimension):

Variation according to:

dialect (The language of a geographical region or of a social class)
time (The language of the eighteenth century, etc.)
province (Language of law, of science, of advertising, etc.)
status (Polite, colloquial, slang, etc., language)
modality (Language of memoranda, lectures, jokes, etc.)
singularity (The style of Dickens, of Hemingway, etc.)

Although not exhaustive, this list indicates something of the range of style differentiation possible within a single language. It is not surprising, perhaps, that we rarely find words which have both the same conceptual meaning and the same stylistic meaning. This observation has frequently led people to declare that 'true synonyms do not exist'. If we understand synonymy as complete equivalence of communicative effect, it is indeed hard to find an example that will disprove this statement. But there is much convenience in restricting the term 'synonymy' to equivalence of conceptual meaning, so that we may then contrast conceptual synonyms with respect to their varying stylistic overtones:

steed (poetic)
horse (general)
nag (slang)
gee-gee (baby language)

domicile (very formal, official)
residence (formal)
abode (poetic)
home (general)

cast (literary, biblical)
throw (general)
chuck (casual, slang)

diminutive (very formal)
tiny (colloquial)
wee (colloquial, dialectal)

The style dimension of 'status' is particularly important in distinguishing synonymous expressions. Here is an example in which the difference of status is maintained through a whole sentence, and is reflected in syntax as well as in vocabulary:

(1) They chucked a stone at the cops, and then did a bunk with the loot.
(2) After casting a stone at the police, they absconded with the money.

Sentence (1) could be said by two criminals, talking casually about the crime afterwards; sentence (2) might be said by the chief inspector in making his official report. Both could be describing the same happening, and their common ground of conceptual meaning is evident in the difficulty anyone would have in assenting to the truth of one of these sentences, and denying the truth of the other.

In a more local sense, social meaning can include what has been called the illocutionary force of an utterance: for example, whether it is to be interpreted as a request, an assertion, an apology, a threat, etc. The function an utterance performs in this respect may be only indirectly related to its conceptual meaning. The sentence *I haven't got a knife* has the form and meaning of an assertion, and yet in social reality (e.g. if said to the waiter in a restaurant) it can readily take on the force of a request such as 'Please bring me a knife'.

From this it is only a small step to the consideration of how language reflects the personal feelings of the speaker, including his attitude to the listener, or his attitude to something he is talking about. Affective meaning, as this sort of meaning can be called, is often explicitly conveyed through the conceptual or connotative content of the words used. Someone who is addressed: 'You're a vicious tyrant and a villainous reprobate, and I hate you for it!' is left in little doubt as to the feelings of the speaker towards him. But there are less direct ways of disclosing our attitude than this: for example, by scaling our remarks according to politeness. With the object of getting people to be quiet, we might say either:

(3) I'm terribly sorry to interrupt, but I wonder if you would be so kind as to lower your voices a little.

or:

(4) Will you belt up.

▷ Consider the view that, when describing social meaning, the number of dimensions that needs to be recognized is potentially endless.

▷ Does 'affective' meaning lend itself to a systematic treatment, as social meaning partly does?

Text 17

LEONHARD LIPKA: *English Lexicology. Lexical Structure, Word Semantics and Word-Formation*. Gunter Narr 2002, pages 116–7

This passage describes the analysis of meanings as a process of breaking down the meaning of a word into its smallest components. As the examples suggest, componential analysis partly resembles the process in mathematics of factorizing a number.

The decomposition of lexemes into semantic elements or components has a long tradition both in European structuralism and American anthropology. In the 1950s anthropologists like W. H. Goodenough applied the componential analysis of meaning to kinship terminology. As far back as 1943, the Danish linguist Louis Hjelmslev argued that words can be analysed into what he called *content figurae*. Some of the examples he gave for such a componential analysis are: *ram* = 'he-sheep', *ewe* = 'she-sheep', *man* = 'he-human being', etc. It has often been noticed that such series of words have certain meaning components in common. These can be made visible by setting up proportional equations and applying the mathematical process of factorizing a number. The following English words are particularly suitable for such a procedure:

(1) *man*   *woman*   *child*
    bull   *cow*   *calf*
    stallion *mare*   *foal*
    ... etc.

To illustrate the process of factorizing a number and its parallel with lexical items, I will use an example given by Leech in slightly modified and simplified form. Just as we can pick out a common factor from a set of numbers, we can extract certain common semantic components from words.

(2)

a)

	4	is to	10
as	6	is to	15
as	8	is to	20
	(2x)		(5x)

b)

	man	is to	*woman*
as	*boy*	is to	*girl*
as	*gander*	is to	*goose*
	(male x)		(female x)

We can easily see the analogy of linguistic and arithmetical proportions. In (2a) the common factors 2 and 5 are picked out, just as in (2b) the components (male) and (female) are extracted. Returning to (1) it is evident that there are common components in both the horizontal and the vertical directions. Represented as a proportional equation (with :: symbolizing the equation) we can say that *man* is to *woman* is to *child* as *bull* is to *cow* is to *calf*. But *man* and *woman* as well as *bull* and *cow* also have something in common as opposed to *child* and *calf*. From these equations we can extract the following factors, components, or features (spelt in capital letters) represented in diagrammatic form:

(3)

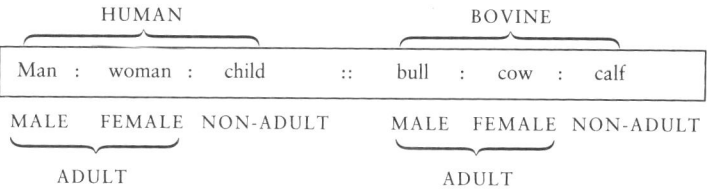

▷ *In parts of the system dealing with species, sex, and adulthood there may be no distinct terms to convey the contrasts. How then do we talk about male and female elephants and their young?*

▷ *What are some of the limitations of describing the semantic relationships between words in terms of 'proportional equations'?*

Chapter 7
Semantics and the dictionary

Text 18
MICHAEL RUNDELL: 'Recent trends in English pedagogical lexicography' in *International Journal of Lexicography* 11/4, 1998, pages 334–5

This passage deals with the impact of corpus data on monolingual learners' dictionaries (MLDs), and especially the influence of corpus-based examples. Ideally, examples should appear uncontrived and natural, and convey a range of grammatical and contextual information.

Probably the most visible way in which dictionaries have changed under the impact of corpus data is the arrival of the corpus-derived dictionary example. There is a certain tension here between the desirability of showing authentic instances of language in use, and the need for examples that work as hard as possible for the user. A. S. Hornby long ago recognized that an invented example could include a range of information types, and pressure on space often requires that a given example sentence should fulfil several functions simultaneously. On the other hand, critics of this approach can point with some justification to the many contrived, unnatural-sounding examples that littered pre-corpus MLDs and could not be seen as reliable models for students to emulate. Despite a certain amount of research into the issue, the jury is still out on the relative merits of corpus-based and lexicographer-produced examples. But it is really no longer relevant to characterize the argument as concerning a simple choice between the authentic and the invented. All reputable MLDs now base every aspect of their text on corpus data, so the differences now lie in the degree to which corpus material is 'processed' on its way into the examples. Compare the following examples for the core meaning of *kill*:

(1) *Careless driving kills. | He was killed with a knife. | Cancer kills thousands of people every year. | We need something to kill the weeds. (ALD5)*

More than 1,000 people have been killed by the armed forces. | Cattle should be killed cleanly and humanely. | The earthquake killed 62 people. | Heroin can kill. (COBUILD2)

Producing successful examples is a deceptively difficult skill, and both sets here do an excellent job. In a necessarily short space, they reveal (among other things):

- grammatical information: *kill* can be transitive or intransitive, and it is often used passively, in which case the agent is marked by *by*, the instrument by *with*
- selectional restrictions: the subject of *kill* is often a human agent, but it can also be an illness, an event, a dangerous drug, or a type of behaviour; the object can be human, animal, or even vegetable
- a range of very typical contexts.

There is not a great deal to choose between these accounts: the *COBUILD* examples have, characteristically, slightly more of the whiff of the corpus about them, but certainly not in a way that could cause any problems for users. Most lexicographers would probably now agree that, where the corpus provides natural and typical examples that clearly illustrate the points that need to be made, there is no conceivable reason for not using them. The risk here, illustrated rather too often in *COBUILD1* but only very occasionally in *COBUILD2*, is that wholly authentic examples can sometimes show mystifyingly irretrievable contexts (for example in *COBUILD1*'s example at *gravitate*: *He gravitated, naturally, to Newmarket*); or too much irrelevant and—to the learner—distracting material.

▷ *The author claims that 'all reputable MLDs [monolingual learners' dictionaries] now base every aspect of their text on corpus data'. In what ways other than by providing authentic examples do corpora improve learners' dictionaries?*

▷ *In the original dictionary entry from which the first block of examples was drawn, verb-pattern 'codes' were placed before the examples, like this: V Careless driving kills./Vnpr He was*

*killed with a knife./Vn Cancer kills thousands of people every
year. (Where 'V' stood for verb, 'n' for noun object, and 'pr'
for preposition.) Do these codes convey information about
verb patterns over and above what the examples convey?*

Text 19

A.P. COWIE: *English Dictionaries for Foreign Learners. A
History.* Clarendon Press 1999, page 167

*Dictionary-makers are now generally careful not to offend
groups of people who are sensitive to particular names or
terms of address. Especially offensive are terms used when
addressing or referring to members of particular religious or
ethnic groups.*

Special awareness and sensitivity needed to be shown when
dealing with words or phrases which imply a disapproving or
offensive attitude towards the person or thing denoted. Precise
guidance had to be given so that students could avoid giving
unnecessary offence through the choice of unsuitable terms.
Three categories of words that needed to be labelled with
particular care were those designated in *ALD 4* as *derogatory,
offensive,* and *sexist.* Derogatory words are those which imply
disapproval or scorn of the person or action referred to (e.g. *slob,
slug, smarmy, swagger*). When used as terms of address (as *slob*
and *slug* can be), they can of course give offence. Particularly
offensive, however, are words such as *dago* or *wop,* used to refer
to or address people, often with the intention of casting a slur
on their religion or ethnic background. These were additionally
marked in *ALD 4* with a 'danger' sign, as follows:

(41) dago ... (! *sl offensive*)

The label *sexist* was introduced for the first time in *ALD 4* as
a means of encouraging greater awareness of the offence which
words such as *bimbo* or *Girl Friday* can cause to women. Its use
went hand in hand with the attempt to be more even-handed in
referring to women in the dictionary and in portraying women
in the full range of occupations and roles which they now fill in
advanced societies. This policy met with some success. As a com-

parative analysis of feminine and masculine nouns and pronouns in examples in parallel sections of *ALD 1* and *ALD 4* has shown, references to females in the fourth edition exceed references to males by a ratio of 7 to 6[1]—and a similar balance is maintained in the fifth.

[1]The ratio was 2 to 1 in favour of males in the first edition.

▷ *The labels used in the text are associated with dictionaries for foreign learners specifically the Advanced Learner's Dictionary (4th edn.). What approach should be adopted when considering their inclusion and labelling in a mother-tongue dictionary?*

▷ *Consider the label 'taboo' as a possible addition to the above set. Again, take account of the type of dictionary when making recommendations.*

Text 20

HENRI BÉJOINT: *Modern Lexicography: An Introduction* (2nd edn.) Oxford University Press 2000, pages 218–9

This extract considers the implications for lexicography of ideas on 'independent' and 'delexical' meaning. It shows that though a word such as 'time' in its 'independent' meaning is relatively infrequent in a large corpus, it will nevertheless tend to be entered before the 'delexical' (and frequent) meanings in many widely used dictionaries.

Sinclair remarks that the most frequent meaning of a polysemous word is very often not an 'independent' meaning, but one which is typically context-bound. For example, the word *time* is relatively infrequent in its 'central' sense in the Birmingham corpus, and most uses of *time* are in more or less petrified expressions ... The most frequent meaning of the form *back* ('in, to, or towards the original starting point, place, or condition') is defined in the *Collins English Dictionary (CED)* at no. 47, whereas no. 1 in the same dictionary ('the posterior part of the human body extending from the neck to the pelvis') is rare in the corpus. Similarly, the most frequent meaning of the verb *pursue* ('to apply oneself to (one's studies, hobbies, interests, etc.)') is no. 5 in *CED*, where no. 1 is 'to follow (a fugitive) in order to capture or overtake', which seems to be much less frequent in discourse. Yet, Sinclair argues, the ordering of meanings in *CED* is not particularly objectionable. It is probably the ordering that any literate native speaker would propose intuitively—and virtually all dictionaries have the same.

The most frequent meanings tend to be more delexicalized than the less frequent ones, just as are the more frequent words compared with the less frequent. The preposition *back* certainly does not have as clear a semantic content as the noun *back*. The verb *pursue* in *pursue one's studies* is strongly delexicalized; the whole phrase is virtually the equivalent (semantically if not stylistically) of *to study*. *Pursue* is a supportive verb just like *take* in *take a look*. All this points towards the following conclusions: the most frequent words, and the most frequent uses of polysemous words, whatever their frequency, seem to tend to have meanings that are less clear, less independent than rarer words, or rarer uses of the same words: meanings tend to lose their autonomy over time and as frequency increases. The highly frequent words like *give, head, heavy, place, time*, etc. are often difficult, or impossible, to define out of the typical contexts in which they occur idiomatically. But when the language users think of a word out of context, it cannot be the delexicalized meaning that comes to their minds first, so that the 'foremost' meaning cannot be the most frequent. Sinclair hypothesizes that it could be 'the most frequent independent sense'.

▷ *The passage suggests that 'meanings tend to lose their autonomy over time and as frequency increases'. What else, in the words themselves and in their contexts, tends to become fixed as time passes and frequency increases?*

▷ *The verb in 'pursue one's studies' is said to be 'strongly delexicalized'. Does this mean that 'pursue' in this sense will collocate very infrequently with other nouns?*

SECTION 3
References

The references which follow can be classified into introductory level (marked ■□□), more advanced and consequently more technical (marked ■■□), and specialized, very demanding (marked ■■■).

Chapter 1
Words and meanings

■□□

GEOFFREY LEECH: *Semantics. The Study of Meaning* (2nd edn.) Penguin 1981 (*see* Text 16)

This introductory text is written in a lucid, attractive style. The first half is partly devoted to exploring issues of language and communication in society, while in the second part Leech presents a theory on principles which have been developed within modern linguistics; one which has strong links with componential analysis.

■■□

ALAN CRUSE: *Meaning in Language. An Introduction to Semantics and Pragmatics* (2nd edn.) Oxford University Press 2004 (*see* Text 3)

This important work, while treating many of the themes covered in the author's *Lexical Semantics* (1986), ranges more widely: there are major sections on grammatical semantics and pragmatics and a chapter which reflects new thinking on word meaning.

■■■

JOHN LYONS: *Linguistic Semantics. An Introduction.*
Cambridge University Press 1995

This is a significant but demanding text, dealing with great rigour with several of the topics discussed in the Survey, including polysemy and homonymy, sense relations, and componential analysis.

Chapter 2
Word-formation

■■□

LAURIE BAUER: *English Word-Formation.* Cambridge
University Press 1983 (*see* Text 2)

This text is divided into two roughly equal sections. In the first, the author deals with a number of theoretical matters, including productivity and grammatical and semantic issues in word-formation. In the second, he provides a detailed description of compounding and derivation.

■■□

P.H. MATTHEWS: *Morphology* (2nd edn.) Cambridge
University Press 1991

This book includes chapters on inflection, derivation, and compounding, with examples drawn from English and other European languages, modern and classical. The theoretical passages are rigorous, lucid, and witty.

■■□

RANDOLPH QUIRK, SIDNEY GREENBAUM, GEOFFREY
LEECH, and JAN SVARTVIK: *A Comprehensive Grammar
of the English Language.* Longman 1985

This, the standard descriptive grammar of English, deals with word-formation in a special Appendix reflecting the view that here is 'an area where grammar and lexicology share a common ground'. The treatment is theoretically broadly-based and accessible to the non-specialist.

Chapter 3
Multiple meaning

■□□

GEORGE LAKOFF and MARK JOHNSON: *Metaphors We Live by*. University of Chicago Press 1980

A readable, non-technical account of an influential theory of metaphor which claims that metaphor is pervasive in everyday life, not just in language but in thought and action, and suggests that conceptual metaphors, for example 'argument is war', structure the arguments we perform when we argue.

■■□

ANDREW ORTONY (ed.): *Metaphor and Thought* (2nd edn.) Cambridge University Press 1993 (*see* Text 8)

This highly stimulating collection of papers explores the themes of metaphor and meaning, metaphor and understanding, and metaphor and science, among others. Especially recommended are the contributions by Lakoff and Reddy (on the 'conduit' metaphor).

■■■

YAEL RAVIN and CLAUDIA LEACOCK: *Polysemy. Theoretical and Computational Approaches*. Oxford University Press 2000

This collection of papers examines polysemy from different theoretical standpoints and in relation to other disciplines, including lexicography and computational linguistics.

Chapter 4
Meaningful relations

■■□

JOHN LYONS: *Semantics. Vol. 1*. Cambridge University Press 1977

This authoritative two-volume work for the advanced student covers a wide range of topics in semantics.

■■□

ALAN CRUSE: *Lexical Semantics*. Cambridge University Press 1986 (*see* Text 11)

Though partly overtaken by the author's *Meaning in Language* (see above), this fully developed treatment of hyponymy, antonymy, and other sense relations, descriptive rather than theoretical in emphasis, is strongly recommended.

Chapter 5
Set phrases

■■□

A.P. COWIE (ed.): *Phraseology: Theory, Analysis, and Applications.* Clarendon Press 1998

This collection represents three areas in phraseology: approaches to the definition of fixed phrases; phraseology in written and spoken texts; and applications of descriptive insights and findings to various fields, including stylistics and lexicography.

■■□

ROSAMUND MOON: *Fixed Expressions and Idioms in English. A Corpus-Based Approach.* Clarendon Press 1998 (*see* Text 12)

This corpus-based description of fixed phrases is remarkable for the light it throws on their frequency, grammatical and discourse functions, and expressive use.

■■□

JOHN SINCLAIR: *Corpus, Concordance, Collocation.* Oxford University Press 1991 (*see* Text 14)

An account of one influential approach to the analysis of collocations in corpus text. The highly original *Cobuild* dictionary is its most significant application.

Chapter 6
Components of meaning

■■□

LEONHARD LIPKA: *English Lexicology. Lexical Structure, Word Semantics and Word-Formation.* Gunter Narr 2002 (*see* Text 17)

This textbook, written in English by a leading German specialist, takes account of current theoretical developments in several semantic areas, and includes treatments of word-formation and phraseology.

■■□
EUGENE NIDA: *Componential Analysis of Meaning*. Mouton 1975 (*see* Text 15)

This classic text by an eminent American linguist and translator adopts a descriptive, non-theoretical approach to componential analysis and is especially skilful at finding elegant solutions to cases involving irregularities.

■■□
ADRIENNE LEHRER: *Semantic Fields and Lexical Structure*. North Holland 1974

The aim of this book is to explore the properties of 'semantic fields'—groupings of words that are closely related in meaning. Insights of field theory include the observation that when some members of a given field acquire figurative senses (as with *boil*, *bake*) others may be semantically extended to join them.

Chapter 7
Semantics and the dictionary

■■□
HENRI BÉJOINT: *Modern Lexicography: An Introduction* (2nd edn.) Oxford University Press 2000 (*see* Text 20)

This is a highly original study, one of its strengths being Béjoint's comparison of the different expectations which different societies or social groups bring to the use of their dictionaries; another is to provide one of the best documented surveys of studies of dictionary use and users.

■■□
SIDNEY I. LANDAU: *Dictionaries: The Art and Craft of Lexicography* (2nd edn.) Cambridge University Press 2001

Now in its second edition, this is an indispensable source of information on dictionary research and compilation, both for the professional lexicographer and the lay reader with an interest in dictionaries. An entirely new chapter deals with the ways in which computer technology has revolutionized lexicography.

■■□

A.P. COWIE: *English Dictionaries for Foreign Learners. A History.* Clarendon Press 1999 (*see* Text 19)

This book traces the history of the foreign learner's dictionary from its sources in programmes of lexical and grammatical research carried out in the 1920s and 1930s, to present-day compilations. Thematic sections deal with the current impact of computer technology and research into dictionary use.

SECTION 4

Glossary

Page references to Section 1, Survey, are given at the end of each entry.

antonymy A type of oppositeness, often involving adjectives and adverbs, whereby if I say 'Mary is older than Jill', I imply 'Jill is younger than Mary'. [9, 37]

back-formation Formation of a new lexical item by the *deletion* of a suffix (or supposed suffix) from an apparently complex word; so 'enthuse' comes by back-formation from 'enthusiasm', and 'burgle' from 'burglar'. [22]

blending The joining together of two words or word-parts, the latter usually being produced by clipping, for example, 'cavalcade' is clipped to '-cade' and then blended with 'motor' to form 'motorcade'. *See* **clipping**. [70]

blocking Said of an existing simple or complex word which, by its existence prevents a synonym from being formed; for example, the prior existence of the verb 'enlist' blocks the use of 'list' as a verb. [17]

branching hierarchy An arrangement in which hyponyms ('potato', 'cassava') form the lowest level, while at the intermediate level 'tuber' acts as superordinate to those items and, at the highest level, as hyponym to 'vegetable'. *See* **non-branching hierarchy**. [44]

chain A linear arrangement of words (or words with particular meanings) with a fixed sequence and a first and last item; as in the sections of a symphonic movement ('exposition', 'development', 'recapitulation', 'coda'). [45]

clipping The cutting away of part of an existing word, for example, 'para-' from 'parachute', which is then blended with an existing word, here 'troops', to form 'paratroops'. *See* **blending**. [70]

collocation (i) A combination, usually of two lexical items in a grammatical pattern, in which one is used in a literal sense and the other in a figurative sense; (ii) the occurrence of two or more words within a short space of each other in a text. [48, 49]

complex word A derivative or compound; also a product of **conversion**. [4, 68]

componential analysis An approach to semantic analysis based on abstract contrastive features, such as 'male', 'female'; 'animate', 'inanimate', etc. [12, 57]

compound A complex word formed by adding one simple word to another. [4, 20]

complementarity A type of oppositeness which has to do with mutual exclusiveness within a single group or area of activity; in the game of chess, the pieces are complementaries because they are either black or white. [39]

connotation The associative, figurative level of language as opposed to the basic conceptual, figurative level. *See* **denotation**. [64]

converseness A type of oppositeness, often involving professional roles or family relationships, whereby if I say 'I am John's tutor', I imply 'John is my student'. [40]

conversion The process by which a lexical item becomes a member of another word-class without the use of a prefix or suffix; also called zero-derivation. [15]

corpus A large body of texts (usually written) stored on a computer. [74]

cycle An arrangement of a set of words in which there is no beginning and no end; every member of the set is arranged between two others, as in the simplest colour circle. [45]

denotation The basic conceptual level of meaning as distinct from the associative level. *See* **connotation**. [64]

derivative A complex word formed by adding an affix (i.e. a **prefix** or **suffix**) to a simple word. [11]

established Acceptance by a speech community that a word or phrase is the appropriate one to use when referring to some object or process. See **lexicalization**. [23]

etymology The study of the origins and history of words. [27]

gradable A quality or process that can be described in terms of 'more' or 'less'; not clear-cut. [65]

gradation A difference between a set of meaning or set phrases, which is not clear-cut but gradual. *See* **scale**. [7]

grammatical item A word belonging to one of the small, finite, and stable classes, such as pronouns and determiners, which interact with lexical items in the construction of sentences. *See* **lexical item**. [5]

ground In metaphor, the perceived similarity between the tenor and vehicle which provides the basis for a comparison (regular backward and forward movement in the case of the 'shuttle' metaphor). *See* **tenor**, **vehicle**. [31]

headword The word, usually in bold print, which stands at the beginning of an entry and is 'looked up' by dictionary users. [26]

homonymy The existence for a given form of two or more quite separate meanings. [7, 25]

hyponymy A semantic relationship of one-to-many, whereby if you say Bill is a spaniel you imply he is a dog (although you don't imply by saying he is a dog that he is necessarily a spaniel). In that example, 'spaniel' is a **hyponym** of 'dog', and 'dog' the superordinate of spaniel. Two or more hyponyms (say, 'spaniel', 'collie') of the same superordinate are its **co-hyponyms**. [9, 40]

idiom A combination of two or more words whose structure is firmly fixed and whose meaning is difficult to determine. *See* **fixed phrase**, **collocation**. [10, 51]

inflectional form A modification of form made to a verb, noun, etc., which serves to indicate differences of tense, aspect, number. [5]

kinship group A family, clan, or other group based on blood relationship. [12]

level of formality The extent to which a piece of written or spoken language indicates closeness or distance between the interlocutors. [64]

lexical field A group of items all of which have a small number of features in common but otherwise have more or less unrelated features. *See* **matrix**. [62]

lexical item A simple word, a derivative, or a compound word. *See* **grammatical item**. [5]

lexicalization The acquisition by a lexical item of a form or meaning which it could not have developed through the application of general rules, for example, the acquisition of the meaning 'designed to carry small children' by the noun 'pushchair'. [15, 16]

main entry One of the divisions of a dictionary, introduced by a **headword** which determines its alphabetical order and containing sub-sections devoted to pronunciation, one or more definitions, examples, etc. [69]

marked One of a pair of contrasting words, say, *vixen, fox*, can be said to be marked if it is more restricted in its use; as *male vixen* is unacceptable, but *male fox* acceptable, *vixen* is marked. *See* **unmarked**. [59, 40]

matrix A grid used in lexical analysis, with the lexical items arranged down one side and the semantic components arranged across the top. [6]

metaphor A figure of speech that consists of combining features of one thing (the 'vehicle') with features of another (the 'tenor') which it resembles in some respect (the 'ground'). [30]

metonymy A figure of speech that consists of using the name of one thing for the name of something else with which it is connected in some respect, for example, 'crown' for 'monarch', 'sail' for 'ship'. [32]

microstructure The internal breakdown of a dictionary entry into definition, examples, etc. *See* **main entry**. [71]

node The central point in a line of text being examined during an analysis using corpus data. [74]

non-branching hierarchy A linear arrangement of items with a fixed sequence and a first and last item. *See* **branching hierarchy**. [44]

onomatopoeic word A word which, like *shatter* and *smash*, is formed from sounds associated with the thing or action it refers to. [4]

open Of the spelling of a compound with the components separated, as in 'town' 'hall'. *See* **solid**. [70]

phraseology That part of the vocabulary of a language which consists of set phrases (i.e. idioms and collocations) and set sentences. [47]

polysemy The existence for a given form of two or more different but related meanings; also multiple meaning. *See* **homonymy**. [7, 12, 25]

prefix A small, meaningful element that cannot occur alone but is attached to the front of a simple word. *See* **suffix**. [15]

productivity The capacity that certain simple words and affixes, and certain rules have to produce a very large number of new items or senses. [69]

rank The way in which positions on a seniority 'ladder', say in the armed forces, are described relative to each other. See 'immediately below X', 'two ranks above Y'. [37]

run-ons A derivative or compound that is positioned *inside* the entry for its chief component (simple word) and usually not defined. [69]

scale A difference between a set of meanings, grammatical classes, etc., which is not clear-cut but gradual. *See* **gradation**. [7]

scale of idiomaticity The gradation along which set phrases are said to be spread out, with fixed and 'opaque' idioms at one end and free and 'transparent' combinations at the other. [10, 55]

semantic feature One of a set of abstract elements, used systematically in various combinations to define individual meanings or sets of meanings. [57]

sense relations The relationships of oppositeness, identity, etc. which exist between specific pairs of items. *See* **antonymy**, **converseness**, **complementarity**. [71]

set phrase A combination of two or more words that is more or less fixed in structure and more or less difficult to interpret; set phrases can be divided into **idioms** and **collocations**. [47]

set sentence An expression, usually a sentence in length and more or less fixed in structure; the category includes such traditional types as proverbs and catchphrases. [9, 48]

simple word A lexical item that can stand alone and that consists of only one meaningful part. *See* **free morpheme**. [4]

slang A special vocabulary used to identify members of a social or professional group and to encourage in them a sense of community. [34]

solid Of the spelling of a compound with the components joined together, as in *lampshade*. *See* **open**. [70]

specialization of meaning A shift of meaning as a result of which a word focuses on one particular aspect of an activity or object (as when *smoke* comes to refer to the habitual aspect of smoking, or its dangers, rather than the activity itself). [30]

speech formula An expression used to convey one's assessment of other speakers and their messages. [49, 54]

spiral A sequence of events (say, the four seasons) with a first word and a last word, and a fixed order, but where after the completion of one circuit, we move forward into the next. [45]

suffix A small, meaningful element that cannot occur alone but is attached to the end of a simple word. *See* **prefix**. [15]

superordinate A word which stands in a relationship of general word to one or more specific words; thus 'dog' is the superordinate of which 'collie' and 'spaniel' are the **hyponyms**. [4]

synonymy A sameness of meaning; note that two or more words may refer to the same object, process, etc. but differ in style, speaker's attitude: for example, 'thin', 'slender', 'skinny'; also, that words are less likely to be synonymous as wholes than in relation to some of their meanings. [8, 35]

tenor The thing or process which, in a metaphor, takes on the characteristics of the vehicle; in the 'caterpillar' metaphor, 'track' is the tenor. *See* **vehicle, ground**. [31]

tree diagram A diagram with a structure of branching, connected lines, representing various objects and relationships. [41]

unmarked One of a pair of contrasting words, say, 'lion', 'lioness', can be said to be unmarked if it is less restricted in its use; as 'male lion' is acceptable, but 'male lioness' not, 'lion' is unmarked. *See* **marked** [59, 40]

vehicle The thing or process which, in a metaphor, is the image chosen to represent and transform the tenor; in the case of the 'shuttle' metaphor, the 'weaver's shuttle' is the vehicle. *See* **tenor**, **ground**. [31]

word-form A modification of form made to a verb, noun, enabling it to indicate differences of tense, aspect, number, etc.; *See* **inflectional form**. [5]

word-formation The production of complex words (chiefly derivatives and compounds). [15]

Acknowledgements

The author and publisher are grateful to those who have given permission to reproduce the following extracts and adaptations of copyright material:

Extracts from 'English word formation' by Laurie Bauer 1983. Reproduced by kind permission of Cambridge University Press.

Extracts from 'Meaning in Language' by A. Cruse, 2004. Reproduced by permission of Oxford University Press.

Extracts from 'Oxford English Grammar' edited by Greenbaum,1996. Reproduced by kind permission of Oxford University Press.

Extract from 'Morphology' by Peter H. Mathews, 1991. Reproduced by kind permission of Cambridge University Press.

Extract from pages 4–6 of 'Introducing metaphor' by Murray Knowles and Rosamund Moon, 2005. Reproduced by kind permission of Routledge.

Extract from 'Metaphor and Thought' by Andrew Ortony, 1994. Reproduced by kind permission of Cambridge University Press.

Extract from 'Semantics: An Introduction to the Science of Meaning' by Stephen Ullmann,1962. Reproduced by kind permission of Blackwell Publishers Ltd.

Extract from 'Semantics' by Frank Robert Palmer, 1981. Reproduced by kind permission of Cambridge University Press.

Extract from 'Lexical Semantics' by D. A. Cruse, 1986. Reproduced by kind permission of Cambridge University Press.

Extract from ' Semantics' by Geoffrey Leech, 1981. Copyright © Geoffrey Leech 1974, 1981. Reproduced by kind permission of Penguin Group UK.

Extract from 'Modern Lexicography' by H. Bejoint, 2000. Reproduced by kind permission of Oxford University Press.

Although every effort has been made to trace and contact copyright holders before publication, this has not been possible in some cases. We apologize for any apparent infringement of copyright and if notified, the publisher will be pleased to rectify any errors or omissions at the earliest opportunity.

牛津语言学入门丛书